A Year at
Clove Brook Farm

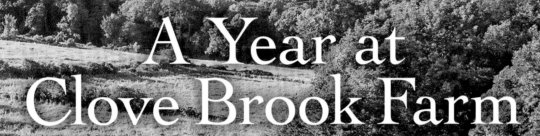

A Year at
Clove Brook Farm

GARDENING, TENDING FLOCKS, KEEPING BEES,
COLLECTING ANTIQUES, AND ENTERTAINING FRIENDS

Christopher Spitzmiller
Foreword by Martha Stewart

WRITTEN WITH CLINTON SMITH
PHOTOGRAPHY BY GEMMA AND ANDREW INGALLS

RIZZOLI
NEW YORK

New York · Paris · London · Milan

I dedicate this book to Albert Hadley, who gave me the confidence to go forward and make all my dreams come true.

And to Anthony Bellomo, who fills every day with more love, encouragement, and patience than I ever could have dreamed of.

TABLE OF CONTENTS

A basket of sweet peas includes white 'Jilly', pink 'Lizbeth', light blue 'Our Harry', and purple 'Winter Sunshine Mauve' varieties.

FOREWORD

By Martha Stewart

Christopher Spitzmiller and I have a lot in common. We both love restoration, renovation, and building from scratch. We both love birds of all types—chickens, pigeons, turkeys, geese, and peafowl—and we often meet at poultry shows, where we purchase the rare and beautiful birds that occupy our dovecotes and henhouses. We both garden in every season, collecting plants and trees and shrubs from here and there and everywhere, filling our cars and trucks with specimens to plant in our ever-expanding landscapes. We both love good food and cooking, amassing the perfect recipes for salad dressings, soufflés, pies, tarts, and bread! We both love to entertain, gathering friends and colleagues in our homes to enjoy the bounty of our gardens and the foods we create in our kitchens. We also both collect antiques and pottery and garden ornaments, sharing our sources and e-mailing photos of recent fabulous finds. And we both center our business efforts on the home, which we both love and cherish, for ourselves as well as for our customers. We are like-minded in many ways, and that is why I like Chris so very much and why we have become such good friends.

But there is another even more important reason that I am so fond of this ebullient and talented man. His industriousness is admirable and obvious to those of us who know him personally. Though he makes it seem effortless, a tremendous amount of thoughtful research, intense planning, and actual sweat and tears go into each undertaking, and his knowledge, whether related to pottery, cooking, gardening, or animal husbandry, is clearly reflected in the completed projects.

I have enjoyed following the thousands of steps Chris took to conceptualize, create, and finally realize this beautiful book and the life depicted herein, and I am looking forward to the next great steps he takes in whatever directions his insatiable curiosity and hard work take him.

INTRODUCTION

On a chilly October day in 2005, while visiting friends in Millbrook, New York, I came across an old white house on a remote country road that was—to be kind—down on its luck. Of course, I immediately fell head over heels for it. I knew instinctively that this run-down property could be transformed into something special, a place that I would be proud to call my home. From that very moment, the house, farm, and adjacent rolling countryside have inspired my dreams, helped me set goals, and, perhaps most importantly, nourished my drive to accomplish it all.

The story of Clove Brook Farm is one of creation—a story that applies to my work as an artist and craftsman as well. For more than twenty-four years, I have produced beautiful handmade ceramic lamps, tableware, accessories, and mirrors that are available in the finest design showrooms and shops throughout the country. I am honored to have made lamps for the four most recent presidential administrations—the Clintons, Bushes, Obamas, and Trumps—a distinction that has earned me the hashtag #PottertothePresidents.

From the beginning, my work and life have been inextricably linked to the earth, its abundant resources, and its endless beauty. As a potter by trade, the essential element of my professional life is clay, which is really nothing more than wet compressed dirt and minerals. Working with my hands to shape and design elements that I am humbled to say have been embraced by my peers has also always meant working with the earth. With Clove Brook Farm, I have found myself taking my passion for creating beauty from clay to creating beauty from the raw materials that surround me here. It's my personal search for perfection in the objects I make and the environments I create that keeps me going. I strive to produce the best of the best, and I have set similarly high standards at the farm for each project that I've tackled, of which there has never been a shortage! One by one,

OPPOSITE: From my first days at Clove Brook Farm until now, the property has certainly evolved, but some things have remained constant, such as my passion for gardening, raising animals, and finding great pleasure in the little things, including setting a beautiful table, even when it's for just two.

I've undertaken the renovations, remodeling, additions to, and redecorating of Clove Brook incrementally, tackling each task as I could pay for it and finishing one before starting another.

This mission took me a good five years with the 2008 recession right in the middle. During that difficult time, I had to stop work on the farm and regroup for a while, but as they say, slow and steady wins the race. There has never been any waiting until the project was "done" to share it with others, though. I entertained happily along the way. All the while, I had friends over to share my progress, have lunch or dinner, and sometimes spend the weekend.

In the midst of one of the most difficult parts of the renovation, my contractor convinced me that I had to re-insulate the house. To accomplish this, all of the walls had to be taken down to the studs, exposing everything. What had been a home—albeit a not-so-glamorous one—was now a shell. I was distraught, but my friend Clare Potter told me, "When the dust is all settled and the bills are all paid, you won't remember any of this and all you will do is enjoy it." She was right.

When the bones of the house were all in place, I called my friend Harry Heissmann, who had once worked with legendary designer Albert Hadley, to help me with the decoration. I had very definite views of what I wanted, but Harry pushed me to look at things differently. The result is so much better because of our collaboration. In planning the renovations at Clove Brook Farm, determination was key; but as with so much in life, luck also played a role. Serendipitously, many things seemed to work out when they needed to, like when some well-preserved eighteenth-century wallpaper fell into my lap at the exact moment that I was finishing my dining room. Later on, during the process of decorating, many pieces of furniture seemed to simply appear at just the right moments, and the interiors continue to evolve. With the help of another friend, I mapped out the dovecote garden, immediately began planting, and haven't stopped since.

I hope this book inspires you to try something new around your own home, whether it's sowing a few fruit and vegetable seeds in a pot or welcoming friends over for a home-cooked dinner. Maybe you'll even try some backyard homesteading with a few chickens. I firmly believe that each of us has a garden within us, and it's our own job to tend to it, nurture it, and let it flourish.

SPRING

MARCH

Truth be told, life at Clove Brook Farm this time of year is quite possibly the most hectic of any of the seasons, but it is also the most exhilarating. Spring presents a unique set of challenges along with endless opportunity. In New York State's Hudson Valley, it is still quite cold in March, even though it is officially spring (at least according to the calendar!). With forecasts that change by the hour, it's the mere promise of what is yet to unfold in the warmer days ahead—after the threat of frost warnings and surprising late-season snowstorms have passed—that keeps me feeling optimistic and forging ahead. For guests who visit the farm in March, things might appear rather still and quiet at first glance, but this seemingly dormant time is actually one of the busiest, as I prepare for all that needs to be done to enjoy a glorious summer garden. Regular maintenance and care, including composting, mulching, fertilizing, and weeding, are ongoing, but I keep the onset of the additional duties that the spring garden requires from becoming overwhelming by mapping out a structured plan, which I follow accordingly. There's definitely a lot to keep me on my toes, and my tattered muck boots are proof of long days spent in the soggy grass. This mapmaking takes time and effort, but the results are revealed in blooms and blossoms and unexpected surprises that delight over the next six months. I try to keep a steady pace throughout this season, so I can really enjoy the fruits of my labor come July and August, when the pool is warm, the dahlias are blooming, and the evenings are perfect for dining alfresco by candlelight.

Perhaps most importantly at this time, one of the things that I really strive for is to make sure that I have given careful thought and consideration to a planting calendar

OPPOSITE: Located in the orchard near the grange hall on my property, my collection of apple trees is among the very first to bloom at Clove Brook Farm. This beautiful mature McIntosh variety offers a profusion of pale pink flowers and chartreuse greenery that I can use for arrangements indoors. PREVIOUS PAGES: Patches of daffodils emerge from the landscape at Clove Brook Farm. Although they look as if they've always been there, all of the groupings were mapped out and planted in a free-flowing manner.

> "Though I do not believe that a plant will spring up where no seed has been, I have great faith in a seed. Convince me that you have a seed there, and I am prepared to expect wonders."
> —*Henry David Thoreau*

that keeps fresh flowers blossoming throughout the coming year. To ensure this, it is imperative that I get a jump start. Bare-root roses I've ordered go into the ground now. (I like to purchase my selections in January so the varieties that I want aren't sold out.) I also begin propagating seeds for annuals in my garage. I adore sweet peas and source heirloom varieties from England, as I have found these easier to germinate than their American counterparts, though they're not much more expensive. I start these around St. Patrick's Day (after soaking the seeds for a minimum of twelve hours); other annuals, such as nasturtiums, cosmos, and zinnias, are started around the same time. May 15 is (allegedly) the last frost date at the farm, which straddles zones 5 and 6 on the U.S. Department of Agriculture's plant-hardiness map. Regardless of where you live, it is recommended to begin your own seedlings indoors six to eight weeks before the last chance of frost in your area. (Check out usda.gov for the plant-hardiness map.) I have friends who are intimidated by the process, but I think it's a great way for beginning gardeners to start developing a green thumb; seeds and grow lights are inexpensive, and it's fun to experiment with plants you've long admired or a color palette that inspires you. As someone who works with his hands in clay every day, there is still nothing like spring, the time of year when I can finally get outdoors, put my hands back in the dirt again, and feel the warmth of the earth and the promise of things to come.

Seed starting, coaxing cuttings to root, and organizing plants are indoor tasks that can be accomplished when spring weather becomes unpredictable. Here, a pair of forced dwarf irises awaits planting. The lemon verbena will soon be sturdy enough to move outdoors once the last chance of frost has passed.

FIRST BLOOMS

Whether it is simple single blossoms in a row of glass tumblers or an oversize vintage urn, basket, or tureen filled with an abundance of branches and flowers, you should never overthink the perfect arrangement. Let the shapes, forms, and textures of what you've gathered inform your direction. The early-blooming lilacs and apple trees at Clove Brook allow me the first opportunity of the year to create something beautiful from my own garden. The combination of the lilac's dense foliage, delicate texture, and heady scent with the gauzy petals of the sturdier apple blossoms is unbeatable. An added bonus: beyond the sheer aesthetic pleasure this dazzling duo brings, these two plants happen to be workhorses in the garden. When I bought Clove Brook, there were a number of extant apple trees that, regrettably, have since died of old age. Soon after moving to the farm, I invested in two fairly large Macoun apple specimens and introduced sixteen other heirloom varieties as saplings. Happily, they have all grown quickly and vigorously. While their aesthetics were a consideration—all the tree's blossoms work well in floral compositions—it was also important to me to choose a mix that would produce apples that were delicious for pie making, cider making, or just eating off the branch. There's a

world of difference in each. Macoun apples are the largest trees I purchased and are appropriate for my region. Their fruit is great for eating right off the tree. I also have Esopus Spitzenburg trees for making cider (a little tart) and Bramley's Seedling (sweeter) for baking. I love their frumpy, idiosyncratic shapes. Cox's Orange Pippin, an English-style apple, and Honeycrisp are great all-around varieties, too.

Lilacs, sophisticated yet simple, cover so many bases. Besides their beautiful, pastel-colored blooms, their romantic, hypnotic scent is literally a breath of fresh air. Getting them to last in a floral arrangement is relatively easy, but it takes a little bit of effort—and some very sharp clippers! Cut them when they are just beginning to open, a quarter to half bloomed. Then, as soon as you have cut the branches, quickly get their tips into a bowl of boiling—yes, boiling—water and let them rest for ten minutes. Then move them to a container of cool water. The branches will have softened and become more pliable. An important note: you must cut an X through the bottom of the branches on the diagonal for them to take in the most water. Cut off as much foliage as you can bear to part with, especially those pieces nearest the flower. The result will be a beautiful assemblage that will last for days and days.

ABOVE: Lilac, an early bloomer, can be used to create long-lasting arrangements. **OPPOSITE**: An oversize composition of branches of apple blossom, 'Sensation' and common lilac, and black fritillaria creates a beautiful focal point in the living room. After working on a large arrangement like this, I pause and revisit it the next day. Once the branches have settled into place, I fill in any holes. To avoid having to deconstruct the arrangement and put it back together when I change the water, I siphon it out with a tube every week.

DOVECOTE GARDEN

One of the first structures I built from scratch at Clove Brook Farm after restoring the main house was a dovecote. With its octagonal shape, remarkable ten-foot-tall vintage windows that I salvaged from a roadside sale for $200, and steep pitched roof, it is one of the most distinctive buildings on the property. Serving as the focal point of my dovecote garden, which contains a mix of annuals, perennials, and topiaries, it is one of my favorite places to experiment. First-time visitors to Clove Brook often make a beeline for the structure, and they are always delighted to discover what lies inside: my rather large family of Indian fantail pigeons. This curious and beautiful variety of bird is to the pigeon family what standard poodles are to dogs—special and showy. While their luminescent plumage—primarily black, with green and purple highlights—is as impossible to describe as the colors in a sunset (it could never be matched to a paint sample),

their broad breasts and fluffy feathered feet are just two of the unique characteristics that set them apart from their fellow feathered friends. In addition to their terrific looks, listening to their sweet coos on a quiet evening brings me to a place of peaceful contemplation.

My attraction to pigeons and desire to create a home for them here at the farm was a long time in the making. I grew up in Buffalo and visited New Orleans and New York City frequently as a child. I was always entranced by city pigeons and the fact that they were fearless, eating cracked corn right out of my hand. Alas, it was not until decades later that I was able to first purchase birds and then breed my own. I have been very pleasantly surprised by how low-maintenance these kind creatures are. A thorough weekly cleaning of the dovecote, plenty of water, and simple feed that I buy from my local farm-supply store is just about all that these lovely birds need to keep them happy and healthy.

ABOVE: Art imitates life at Clove Brook Farm. My real-life fowl populations mimic the stance of an antique fantail pigeon garden ornament, one of a pair in the garden. **OPPOSITE**: The dovecote is a focal point of the dovecote garden, which has a succession of different plantings throughout the year. In the early spring, a mix of bold tulips adds an air of informality to the symmetrical layout and sculpted boxwoods that define the garden's crisp borders. I designed the dovecote so that it would complement the farm's other nineteenth-century Greek Revival structures. Tall triple hung windows allow breezes to flow through for the birds, and an antique lead weather vane featuring a pigeon taking flight adds a decorative flourish.

OPPOSITE: My flock includes black Indian fantail, blue Indian fantail, and other mixed fancy pigeon breeds. Their soft cooing sounds waft through the garden and have a lulling effect. Along my fencerow, I found a tree with an ungainly shape but lots of limbs—the even spacing of which made them ideally suited for the dovecote's tall and narrow space, as well as giving the birds plenty of room to perch. **ABOVE**: Blue Indian fantail pigeons are renowned for the deep, lustrous colors of their feathers, as well as the unique markings on their wings.

Anchored by a sea of tulips and fritillaria, each of the four garden beds in the dovecote garden features tall, obelisk-shaped iron *tuteurs* for architectural interest. Climbing 'Eden' roses spring to life later in the season and envelop them.

OPPOSITE: Young geese, known as goslings, will bond with their owners and follow them around. Mine are no exception, and love to trail behind me on my walks around Clove Brook!
ABOVE: Although extremely charming and endearing, older geese sometimes exhibit loud squawking and can be aggressive if their space is infringed upon. My Sebastopol and Embden breeds are able to roam freely during the day (and take a dip in the pool), which seems to contribute to their even-temperedness. At night, they are kept in a coop with an outdoor run to protect them from predators.

APRIL

O h, the joy of April and, at last, signs of life on the farm! Clove Brook becomes a hive of activity at this time of year. While March is filled with many tasks and my to-do list continues to grow, it's in April that I begin to see the result of my quiet efforts and diligence over the course of the preceding months. The ground has thawed, the grass is green, and suddenly I'm like a kid on Christmas morning. It is in April that two of my favorite plants bloom—by the thousands. I love daffodils and narcissi, and from my bedroom window on a chilly morning, I can see parts of the farm transformed into veritable carpets of the ethereal blooms. There are thousands of varieties of daffodils and narcissi, but I have been decisive about what I want to include in my gardens. As gorgeous as the yellow varieties pictured in the pages of the dozens of garden mail-order catalogs I receive are, I forgo the bolder, brighter varieties in favor of softer white and cream ones with the palest of pale yellow or orange centers. These subtle variations in hue create delicately shaded masses of color that make me think of clouds floating by. It was important to me that these flower beds have a look that is as naturalistic as possible, yet such nonchalance is not left to chance. What appear to be freely formed patches that have evolved over the years are actually a result of the meticulous planting of a thousand bulbs every year over the past five years. First-time visitors to Clove Brook think these flowers have always been here, which is the ultimate compliment, but the process hasn't been without trial and error. Originally, I planted the bulbs in a very structured way, row upon row, but I soon discovered (five months after they went into the

A basket of 'Sir Winston Churchill', 'Stainless Steel', 'Geranium', and 'Pheasant's Eye' daffodil specimens.

31

"What I have ever sighed for has been to retreat to a Swiss farm, and live entirely surrounded by cows—and china." —*Charles Dickens*

ground and began to sprout) that this look was far too rigid. Now, amorphous patches here and there dot the landscape like marshmallows, particularly down by the pond. From the kitchen porch, one's eye is drawn to their fleeting blooms, which create a lovely axis and focal point. Getting these beauties to grow is easy, but my preparations begin the previous October when new bulbs arrive at the farm. These have to be in the ground before Thanksgiving so they have a sufficient chilling period. If you prefer a nice and tidy formal garden, keep the daffodils relegated to a peripheral area. You have to let them die back before cutting them down, which isn't until mid-July. For those three months, they might not look so tidy.

If thousands of bulbs aren't in your gardening plan, one of my favorite things to do is to "force" them to bloom inside, a rewarding practice that any novice can tackle—kids love it, too. The scent is worth it, even if you grow just one or two. Make no mistake: April showers bring a newfound life and energy to the farm—as evidenced by the muddy paw prints of my two dogs, Fanny and Lyon, everywhere—yet I am giddy with anticipation knowing that the garden's finest moments of the year are just around the corner.

Atop my kitchen fireplace mantel, an arrangement of 'Sir Winston Churchill' daffodils exudes a magnificent fragrance. When I display the flowers, I always retain some of the plant's sinuous leaves for added interest; otherwise, the composition can feel too stalky and stiff.

EASTER

I always make a silent wish for a mild, perhaps even warm, Easter, but if there is still a brisk chill in the air, it does nothing to dampen my spirits. Easter is among my favorite holidays and one that I love to share with friends. I try to make this day as special as I can, but also with as little fuss as possible, and my garden provides me with just about everything I need to do that. On the day before Easter, I begin my morning in the chicken coop to gather what I know will be a beautiful mix of eggs from my Araucana, Copper Marans, Buff Orpington, Barred Rock, and Coronation Sussex chickens. The color of their eggs will range from bright whites and creamy browns to icy blues and pale greens—no dyes needed! Devoted as I am to my lively and animated flock, I also love chickens of the faux variety. Over time, I have assembled a vast collection of vintage pressed- and milk-glass lidded chicken dishes, decorative yet functional objects that are pressed into service for this special day. After gathering the daffodils and narcissi from the yard, I reach into my cupboards for distinctive vessels to hold the bouquets. I usually start with one of my coveted pieces of Dodie Thayer Lettuce Ware. Never use floral foam—you should opt instead for black-coated chicken wire rolled into a ball and placed at the bottom of your vessel. (The coating on the wire keeps it from scratching, and since it is reusable, it's also environmentally friendly.) If I still have snowdrops blooming, they too will find their way into one of my arrangements. Once the flowers are in place, I bake a ham for three hours with a brown sugar–and–apricot jam glaze. A potato gratin, asparagus from the garden that's grilled and seasoned with salt, pepper, lemon, and olive oil, plus a simply dressed salad are all that's needed to round out a perfect holiday meal.

People are sometimes surprised to learn that I am absolutely not afraid to outsource part of the meal for a large gathering. If you trust your guests' cooking or the purveyors they regularly shop, don't be shy in asking them to bring dessert or whatever you wish. Interior designer Ashley Whittaker, my friend and neighbor, is always game to bring a divine coconut cake—sometimes in the shape of a bunny or a lamb! Other friends also offer and inquire ahead of time, and I like to take people up on their generosity. After all, they wouldn't ask if they weren't willing to do it. At last, when it comes time for the egg hunt for the young ones, plastic golden eggs containing candy and dollar bills are hidden throughout the garden. Despite their desirability, undiscovered eggs inevitably continue to be found throughout the year. Easter is, indeed, the holiday that keeps on giving!

ABOVE: Eggs from my Araucana, Copper Marans, Buff Orpington, Barred Rock, and Leghorn chickens provide a beautiful palette for a centerpiece—no dyeing required! OPPOSITE: The cobalt hen roosting on her nest is part of a larger collection of vintage pressed glass. I love how the color plays off of the amethyst goblets. The 'Sir Winston Churchill' daffodils are what's known as a double variety and feature clusters of cream petals and a saffron-colored heart.

My Easter table is dressed
up with some of my favorite
linens, china, and glassware.
While the garden hasn't quite
filled in with dense foliage, the
eighteenth-century wallpaper's
lush scenic landscape gives
the room a springlike air.

THIS PAGE: Fresh-picked asparagus needs minimal preparation beyond a quick turn on the grill and a little seasoning of salt, pepper, olive oil, and lemon juice. **OPPOSITE, CLOCKWISE FROM TOP LEFT:** Tender stalks await harvesting. A bunch is ready for the grill. Although they look delicate, late-blooming 'Summer Snowflakes' are some of the heartiest bloomers (some varieties emerge while there's still snow on the ground). A white primrose features a rosette of large, textured deep green leaves.

MAY

It's showtime at Clove Brook, and the pace of the next couple of months is like running a marathon. The rewards of months of planning and preparation are finally starting to pay off as the garden springs to life, a result of warmer days and, hopefully, the April showers that encouraged things along. It's my hope that everything comes together as imagined in my head, although I don't take any of it for granted. The seedlings that I've nurtured in the garage are ready to be planted at the end of the month—and quickly! The chicks are also hatching now. And the peonies are starting to put on a spectacular show with their colorful blooms, as vivid as a fireworks display.

Most importantly, the race is on to procure unique and unusual plants at some of my favorite nurseries and plant fairs. Friends know that the third weekend of May is like Christmas to me, because it's the annual Trade Secrets event in nearby Litchfield County, Connecticut. For one day only, rare plants and garden furnishings are for sale at this lauded fair, while a second day is devoted to garden tours at nearby private estates. I've been attending for several years. At the last few, I've been at the front of the line for the early-bird shopping that starts at 8:00 A.M. This group of attendees is serious!

I often joke with friends that they cannot talk to me during those wee hours, as it's a sprint from one vendor to the next to make selections and purchases before someone else snaps up a treasure. Most of the furniture and accessories are one-of-a-kind vintage or antique pieces, so you can't be indecisive. Similarly, some exhibitors only have a few plants of a certain variety for sale. You might not see the likes of them again until the

OPPOSITE: My garage porch offers not only the perfect perch for relaxation, but also is the ideal spot for my collection of myrtle, cypress, and coleus topiaries. Sheltered from the harsh midday sun, which can stress them, they seem to thrive there atop the Victorian wire plant stand. The vintage rattan chaise and wicker chair belonged to my grandparents.

following year—if ever—and you probably won't come across them at your neighborhood nursery. Over the years, I've developed some amazing relationships with growers from as far away as Maine who exhibit here, and I stay in touch with them throughout the year to know what they will be bringing for each fair. I love growing beautiful auriculas (also called auricula primroses), but the finicky alpine plants can also be difficult to source. At a Trade Secrets event several years ago, I met a nursery owner who specializes in them, and they now let me know in advance what varieties they'll be selling.

May is also the time that I map out my herb beds at Clove Brook and get them planted accordingly; I prefer to start over each year as the flavor can change year to year in herbs that come back. It's also the time to execute any sort of major (and minor) hedge, tree, or shrub planting, whether it's to replace any specimens I lost over the winter or define a new garden area on the property. If the weather is agreeable, proper outdoor entertaining is on the calendar once again, and I love to create arrangements where my peonies can bask in their glory. May is a reminder that summer is just around the corner, and I plan on making the most of every second.

Antique concrete squirrel garden ornaments flank the entrance to the dovecote garden. Their winsome demeanors add a touch of whimsy and offer a cheerful welcome.

PEONY LUNCHEON

My love for peonies is unwavering, so much so that I've immortalized them in a series of hand-thrown plates I designed that feature ones I've grown at Clove Brook Farm. Together with my studio team, I photograph the blooms in a small white-box studio in the grange hall on my property. They are then put on a ceramic transfer, which is like a decal or tattoo, and applied to the plates. These plates are fired at a much lower temperature than other ceramics. We played with the scale for a long time and ended up with a look that we like and that customers responded to with enthusiasm. The success of those plates has, in turn, inspired the creation of two additional sets of flower plates: the aforementioned peonies, plus a sweet pea and dahlia collection.

For this gracious Saturday lunch in my field, I surrounded the table with vintage chairs from my great-grandparents' house along the Canadian shore of Lake Erie. Covering the table was a new tablecloth that features a classic Tillett Textiles print favored by Bunny Mellon and Billy Baldwin. I happened upon forty never-used napkins in this same Tillett pattern at an auction of Mellon's home furnishings, and a friend gifted me the matching tablecloth. I sent most of the napkins to friends but kept a few for myself. I love the juxtaposition of the pale blue Leontine Linens napkins with the bold red monogram in a block script set against the flowery tablecloth.

The real joy of this table, besides the ebullient peony blooms, comes from the assortment of petite accents. The silver shovels and salt spoons may not be one-of-a-kind pieces, but they are certainly conversation starters, just as the frogs and ladybug ornaments inspire delight and add a touch of whimsy that often seems to be missing from contemporary tablescapes. There are also objects that I search for more actively. I have thousands of napkins and a small army of place mats, but it's not a stellar bounty. You could say that I'm napkin rich and place-mat poor! I love the contrast and juxtaposition of mixing and matching linens, but it takes patience to build a collection.

ABOVE: The rich crimson color of a 'Cherry Charm' peony is always a standout in the garden. **OPPOSITE**: For a luncheon on the lawn, I selected one of my favorite tablecloths that I had custom printed by Tillett Textiles in Sheffield, Massachusetts. The butterfly and floral pattern was a favorite of gardener and philanthropist Bunny Mellon. The chairs belonged to my great-grandparents and came from their home along the shores of Lake Erie. **FOLLOWING PAGES**: A bounty of peonies, lilacs, and viburnums rest in faux-bois cachepots of my own design. **PAGES 48–49**: The vase of baby chicks is a temporary gesture and they are returned to the brooder when the meal begins.

ABOVE: A border of pink and red peonies graces the perimeter of the pool garden. They are mixed in with a variety of lilies, which will begin blooming soon after the peonies fade. **OPPOSITE**: The plates feature photographs of peonies from the garden that were fired onto the clay through a transfer process. Bud vases hold individual stems. **FOLLOWING PAGES**: A selection of peonies grown at the farm.

Christophe

'SEIDAI' TREE

'ABALONE PEARL'

'BUCKEYE BELLE'

'SOFT SALMON JOY'

'CORAL SUNSET'

'LIEBCHEN'

'MAGENTA GEM'

'FIRST ARRIVAL' ITOH

'MARTHA'

'BURMA JOY'

'CORAL CHARM'

'LAVENDER WHISPER'

'CYTHEREA'

'MORNING LILAC' ITOH

'CLOWN'

'FESTIVA MAXIMA'

'FAIRVIEW'

'ATHENA'

THIS PAGE: To prolong peony blooms, I condition them by removing most of their leaves except what's closest to the flower. I also keep them in a cool spot out of direct sunlight. OPPOSITE, CLOCKWISE FROM TOP LEFT: A sharp pair of steel garden scissors are ideal for cutting small branches and removing excess leaves. 'Newport' viburnum is a perfect complement to peonies. I cut each stem at an angle so it can absorb the most water. A reusable ball of coated chicken wire anchors the arrangement.

BABY CHICKS

In late May and early June, I usually welcome a few dozen baby chicks to Clove Brook. Their sweet chirps add a joyful noise to the farm, and because I raised chickens when I was young, the annual hatching is a really meaningful event that brings me fond recollections of my childhood. The chicks have been hatched from eggs that I collected from my hens back in February and are kept in a brooder in the grange hall for the first few weeks of their development. Breed standards dictate what is considered a "perfect" bird, such as its size, body shape, and even the number of points on its crown. I primarily breed Buff Orpingtons for their even temperament and proficient egg-laying capabilities, but also Araucanas for their beautiful pale blue and green eggs.

I hatch about thirty chickens a season, but before we can touch their soft feathers, the eggs are kept in an incubator for twenty-one days at a constant 99.5 degrees Fahrenheit for development. An automatic roller turns them every hour to help them develop. Once they've hatched, they are first moved to a large empty aquarium where I can keep an eye on them from all sides; a heat lamp overhead protects them from cold drafts.

After a couple of weeks, they're moved to a bigger brooder for more space, and that usually promotes the growth of healthier chickens that also grow faster than those kept confined to tight areas. I enjoy their peeps and chirps indoors as long as I can, and after six to eight weeks they're moved into a safe area in the barn with chickens of similar size and temperament.

OPPOSITE: Buff Orpingtons are a nineteenth-century winter-hardy breed known for their docile temperaments, large stature, and proficient egg production. They are stately birds recognized by their fluffy feathers, which are soon evident after they've hatched. **ABOVE**: In their brooder—a repurposed aquarium lined with paper towels—week-old Buff Orpingtons find their traction.

Strawberry Rhubarb Jam   Makes 7 Pints

8 Cups Local Fresh Strawberries Hulled
                                    if Large 1/2 - if Small Whole
10 Cups Rhubarb Cut into 3/4 inch Pieces
7 Cups Granulated Sugar
1/4 Teaspoon Salt
2 TBS Lemon Juice
2 TBS Lemon Zest
1 TBS Rose Water

In a Large Dutch oven Combine the Strawberries Rhubarb, Sugar, Salt, Lemon Juice and Zest. Heat on Medium High, Stirring every 5 mins until the Mixture Rattles 220° On a Candy Thermometer. The Jell Set Point. Keep at this temp for 10 mins. The Mixture should be thick + Jell a little on a Cooled Wooden Spoon

When the Jam Cools Slightly but is still Hot add the Rose Water, Place in Sterilized Jars Wipe Rim, Well, important, Place Lids + Screw Tops on Jars and tighten to 'Finger tight' Place Jam Jars in Boiling Water 'Submereged' at Least 2" for 10 mins at a Rolling Boil The Lids Shouldn't indent as they Cool overnight If they don't indent - Refrigerate + Use First Store the Jars in a Cool Dark Place - Basement ideally. For up to 1 Year.

Label + Date Your Jars.

RHUBARB

I love rhubarb, and I love to combine it with other ingredients. From the moment rhubarb begins to burst from the garden, it gives and gives and gives and can be harvested until the end of the season. This time of year, locally grown strawberries are at their peak—so naturally sweet that they don't need sugar—and they become available just as the rhubarb is ready for harvest. One of my favorite recipes is a simple strawberry-rhubarb jam that is a time-tested crowd favorite. It's great to serve guests, and it also makes for a lovely hostess gift when presented in pretty jars.

Rhubarb can be either red or green in color, and the flavor is equally good in both. And while the stalk is delicious, the plant's foliage is toxic to humans and should be avoided. With its striking color and unique tart flavor, rhubarb is my go-to for a variety of dishes, syrups, sauces, and purees. Besides the jam I make, rhubarb is perfect for pies and crisps and great in fizzy drinks and cocktails.

If you have a friend who can propagate rhubarb for you from an established plant—which is as easy as dividing a crown with a bud—that's an ideal way to jump-start your own crop the same year. Otherwise, a small planting from a nursery can take a good three years to produce any yield. But don't fret: your patience is worth the future payoff.

OPPOSITE, CLOCKWISE FROM TOP LEFT: Rhubarb's striking, colorful stalks. My handwritten recipe for making rhubarb-and-strawberry jam. Jars ready to be sealed. The plant's rich colors and texture make it both a visual and a tasty treat. **ABOVE**: Rhubarb, fresh from the garden.
FOLLOWING PAGES: Ingredients for my rhubarb crisp, including brown sugar, butter, and oats for the crumble topping, are mise en place, making preparation easy with everything at hand.

DIGGING AND PLANTING

It may seem surprising that of the many eye-catching gestures I have created in the garden, all of them can be attributed to the help of just a few simple, basic, and widely available tools. First, I would be lost without the thousands of wooden stakes that I buy to label all of my plantings—those I can see, of course—but especially those bulbs, tubers, and seeds that are dormant for long periods before sprouting. Not only do I label the type of plant, I often note its color, particularly if there are multiple varieties. As much as I'd like to think I can remember what has been planted where, one can easily lose track once the pots they came in have been discarded and the seeds in the ground have been covered with dirt. I always use bamboo rods or wooden stakes and jute twine, all of which are biodegradable.

A variety of trowels proves to be indispensable, as each one serves a different purpose—the pointy ones are perfect for planting seedlings and working in rocky soil; the wide ones are ideal for planting bulbs. Supersharp clippers from Japan are kept handy for pruning small, low-hanging branches, and as much as I like to get my hands in the dirt, a good pair of gloves keeps me safe from cuts and splinters. I buy multiple pairs of inexpensive, good-quality gloves that can be thrown in the washer and air-dried and kept around the various parts of the property—on the terrace, near the dovecote, in the garage, and at the pool house. Because the gardens at Clove Brook are so spread out, I like to know that there's always a clean, dry pair nearby and ready at a moment's notice.

ABOVE: Basil seedlings await planting with a slim trowel. The plants have tender roots and will succumb to late spring cold snaps and should be planted well after any signs of frost in the forecast. **OPPOSITE**: Wide trowels with curved sides are ideal for shoveling, scooping, and weeding. Trowels with long, thin blades and a pointed tip aid in transplanting. Small, scissorlike clippers are used for snipping rosebuds or poppy blooms. For heavy pruning, a pair of hand shears with a large blade can cut through thick branches. Clippers with long blades are helpful for shaping large swaths of shrubs, such as lilacs. Wooden plant labels, bamboo stakes, and jute twine are all biodegradable, and rubber gloves get washed and reused regularly.

ABOVE: Once the tulips have finished blooming, the second planting of the season takes place in the dovecote garden. Kale, zinnia, and nasturtium plants were all started from seed. **OPPOSITE**: After the spent tulips and their bulbs have been removed, the soil must be tilled and loosened for the next succession of plantings. The sweet peas have already started climbing the crisscross wattle fencing and will cover it by June.

Spring Calendar

MARCH

Plant bare-root roses and sweet peas in the garden. Fertilize roses every month through July.

Start annual seeds indoors under grow lights.

Turn the compost pile, which should be done once a month.

Prepare incubator for chicks one week before setting eggs. First chickens begin to hatch.

Move tropical plants outside during warm daylight hours.

Plan herb-garden layout.

Spread compost and fertilizer over dovecote garden.

Create large flower arrangements with apple blossoms and lilac branches.

Photograph the garden every month. Print and date the pictures for future reference.

APRIL

Plant dahlia tubers.

Trim back any deadwood on roses. Prune thoroughly—the plants thrive on new growth.

Sow seeds of cold-hardy vegetables and flowers—such as lettuces, snap peas, zinnias, and nasturtiums—outdoors.

Bring lawn furniture outdoors from winter storage.

Shop for both new and vintage outdoor furnishings and accessories. I love the surprises I find at the New York Botanical Garden's Antique Garden Furniture Fair.

Two weeks before the holiday, order a ham for Easter brunch.

Remove winter storm windows and install screens.

Plant fruit trees.

Remove sod in preparation for any new garden spaces, and relocate grass to areas with spotty coverage.

Spread a generous layer of mulch on flower beds to avoid laborious weeding later.

MAY

Uncover the pool on May 1.

Order next year's tulip bulbs while this year's are blooming.

Mid-month, start planting the flower beds, being careful not to overcrowd. Even with six-inch spacing between each, plants will fill in quickly.

Attend local plant sales. Trade Secrets is always top of my list.

Visit your favorite garden centers and make time to discover new ones.

Make rhubarb pies and jams.

Harvest the last asparagus by mid-May.

GIFT OF THE SEASON
Every season, I have a go-to item for gift giving from the farm. In the spring, my homemade strawberry-rhubarb jam is the perfect accompaniment to morning toast and buttery scones.

SPRING RECIPES

RHUBARB PIE

I was given this recipe by my friend John Rosselli, but I think I improved it by adding more topping—just don't tell him!

FOR THE PIE:

1 pie crust, homemade or store-bought

4 cups chopped fresh rhubarb or frozen rhubarb, thawed

⅔ cup granulated sugar

1 tsp. ground cinnamon

Juice of half a lemon

3 Tbsp. all-purpose flour

FOR THE TOPPING:

4 cups Smart Start or Corn Flakes cereal

½ tsp. ground cinnamon

½ stick salted butter (4 Tbsp.), at room temperature

¼ cup dark brown sugar, firmly packed

1. Preheat oven to 375°F.

2. Roll out pie crust, place in a 9-inch round glass pie plate, and refrigerate until dough is firm.

3. Cut rhubarb into ¾-inch pieces and toss with sugar, cinnamon, lemon juice, and flour. Put mixture in chilled pie crust.

4. Prepare ingredients for topping. Crush cereal in a medium mixing bowl, then add the cinnamon, butter, and brown sugar. Mix with your fingers until you have a rough crumble.

5. Spread topping evenly over pie filling, cover with aluminum foil, and bake for 45 minutes. Uncover and bake 15 more minutes, or until crumble is golden and filling is bubbling.

6. Serve hot, warm, or room temperature with vanilla ice cream.

COLD-BREW BLACK TEA WITH FRESH MINT

I like to see the stems of mint protruding above the top of the pitcher—it just looks festive.

4 pints cold or room-temperature water

1 large black tea bag, preferably Luzianne

1 bunch fresh mint

1. Fill a pitcher with water.

2. Place tea bag in pitcher along with bunch of fresh mint. Steep tea for approximately 30 minutes.

3. Serve over ice.

COLD-BREW GREEN TEA WITH MINT, LEMON BALM, OR LEMON VERBENA

4 pints cold or room-temperature water

3 green tea bags, preferably Tazo

1 bunch fresh herbs of your choice

Follow directions for black tea above.

LEMON VERBENA TEA

No caffeine, no calories, refreshing, and great for digestion and relaxation. The process below also works really well with fresh mint.

1 large bunch fresh lemon verbena

Large heatproof pitcher or glass carafe

1. Place bouquet of lemon verbena in pitcher.

2. Pour boiling water over bundle, and let steep until cool. Serve over ice.

SUMMER

JUNE/JULY

The unofficial start of summer for many folks is Memorial Day weekend. The sandy shores and beaches of Long Island Sound are less than sixty miles from the rich, fertile soil of Millbrook, yet seemingly a world away. At Clove Brook, our last frost date is almost always around May 15, so lounging poolside comes several weeks after most people get a jump start on the sunny season. I gleefully revel in these early chilly plunges into the deep end of the pool, but not all of my guests share the same joy in these invigorating dunks into—some say cold, I say bracing—water, but most are game to try . . . at least once!

After we get the all-clear from the weather gods, the *Farmers' Almanac*, and the local meteorologists from Albany who declare that frost won't return until October, there is immediately a scurry to get both mature plants and fledgling seedlings into the ground as soon as possible—a routine that continues well into late June. Even with my meticulous planting schedules and years' worth of gardening journals to reference, that flurry of activity, just short of chaos, is stimulating and very exciting. If I lay the groundwork correctly, I know that my friends, family, and I will benefit greatly from several months of joyful blooms, such rewards exponentially outweighing the efforts exerted.

I do not have a greenhouse, but luckily I am not daunted by the time-consuming process of moving hefty containers and fragile plants in and out (and in and out) of the garage over several weeks to slowly acclimate and strengthen them. It seems that each season I still learn something new about how much chilly weather the delicate foliage of my tropical plants and citrus trees can withstand. Thankfully, not everything goes into the ground at the same time. My sweet peas, which were planted back in March, are just

70

> *"One touch of nature makes the whole world kin."*
> —*William Shakespeare*

now beginning to bloom. I work on coaxing their delicate, sinuous tendrils to grab onto the burlap twine supports that I've created for them, as I enjoy the benefit of the fragrance they bring. (The burlap is completely biodegradable—no plastic twist ties here.)

The 'Annabelle' hydrangeas on the warmer west side of the house also begin to light up, their abundant blooms ready to burst open at a moment's notice. The 'Annabelle' has always been a particular favorite of mine. Not only are they showstoppers, but their early-season blooms ensure that I will have the cut flowers I crave after so many months of dormancy.

Up by the pool, the poppy seeds that I planted around St. Patrick's Day begin to open one by one—each bloom is an explosion of color and wily, ruffled textures. Some are black, some red, and others are deep, dark purple; there are a number that even look like carnations. Every year, they cross-pollinate, and I'm always surprised by new blooms that I've never seen before and probably won't see again. I let Mother Nature lead the way and simply enjoy them while they last.

There is a saying, "Life is 95 percent maintenance." As we move into July, the needs of the garden require a little less of my attention. Thankfully, my initial planning has kept it all from becoming overwhelming. The more I do and the more I learn, the less time-consuming these maintenance tasks become, which leaves me with even more opportunities to experiment with different planting schemes, unique color combinations, and plants I've yearned to grow. Yes, my weekends are busy staking dahlias, cutting the grass, and weeding the herb garden, but the end result is always worth the effort.

The 'Our Harry' sweet pea is sweetly scented, and its special blue color—which varies from periwinkle to lavender, depending on the light of the day—makes it a standout in the garden. I start seedlings in the garage ten to twelve weeks before the last frost, and plants can grow up to eight feet tall.

DINING ON THE TERRACE

On the occasions I decide to serve a late-afternoon lunch instead of going out to dine, I rely on tried-and-true classic recipes that don't heat up the kitchen or keep me from my guests for prolonged periods of time. I often welcome an extra set of hands in the kitchen, and folks are always more than eager to pitch in, either with prep work or setting the table. The latter shouldn't require too much fuss, so I sometimes eschew a tablecloth on the terrace table when it's just a casual get-together. My assortment of colored green glassware is always a favorite addition, as is my vintage bamboo flatware and star-shaped raffia place mats topped with my hand-thrown sweet pea plates. I never shy away from using an unexpected mix of textures and colors on a table. In lieu of a large floral arrangement, an overscale ceramic gourd that I designed serves as the centerpiece; a scattering of tiny bud vases filled with poppy blooms add just the right touch of natural adornment. Once the scene is set and we make our way from the kitchen to the table, a green salad tossed in a light aioli serves as a simple starter, while a salmon pan-seared in my cast-iron skillet is also a quick and easy main course. But the shallots I roast in duck fat are the real crowd-pleaser. It's rare that a side dish can be the star of the show, but shallots are often overlooked, and I like putting a unique—not to mention tasty and indulgent— twist on a humble ingredient. We finish the meal with beautiful chocolate meringues topped with whipped cream, milk chocolate flakes, and a garnish of fresh mint from the garden. Then it's time for a nap.

ABOVE: A vintage frog by French ceramist Jean Roger, one of a pair, adds a whimsical touch to the terrace console. **OPPOSITE**: A potted agave on the console and a cycad in the antique cast-iron urn add a subtle tropical vibe to this outdoor luncheon. A ceramic gourd vessel that I designed serves as the centerpiece. **FOLLOWING PAGES**: My extensive collection of original Dodie Thayer Lettuce Ware pottery lines a shelf in the kitchen and is used regularly, not just for special occasions.

ABOVE: Star-shaped raffia place mats are a nice change from round or square ones, particularly when I don't use a tablecloth. The sweet-pea plates are one of my studio designs, and the bamboo flatware belonged to Jacqueline Kennedy Onassis. **OPPOSITE, CLOCKWISE FROM TOP LEFT**: Salmon is seasoned, ready to be grilled, and the salad awaits dressing—preparation is kept simple on hot summer days. Roasted shallots. Milk chocolate flakes, whipped cream, and a mint garnish adorn the meringues. The meringues get a light dusting of unsweetened cocoa powder.

HYDRANGEA HEAVEN

I love hydrangeas. I admire their massive blooms and the stately presence they bring to the garden, as well as their versatility and adaptability—they ask very little of you in terms of maintenance. Even novices can plant one large hydrangea in a big container and call it a day. Flank a door with two to create a real sense of arrival with little effort. Each plant can have its own "wow" moment. 'Annabelle' is the very first bloomer. 'Snow Queen' oakleaf hydrangeas show up next. The herbaceous borders along the front of my house are mid-season bloomers—think 'Limelight', peegee, and 'Tardiva'. 'Endless Summer' blue varieties are sprinkled here and there. (I find the white bloomers to be much heartier.) Climbing hydrangeas claw their way to the top of my chimneys and a few specimen trees and possess spectacular lacy flowers. They are slow to get

established, but they take off like a rocket after a couple of seasons. For the most part, they are not intrusive like some climbing ivies or creeping vines with invasive tendril roots.

To be completely candid, hydrangeas offer a lot of bang for the buck. I have perhaps seventy-five of the 'Limelight' variety, and their output is bountiful. They provide armful after armful of flowers that you can dry at season's end. I keep a lot, but I also gift them to friends. As difficult as it is to resist, I'm very reluctant to cut them when they're still blooming, as I know I can only get about four days of immediate gratification from them in a vase before they start to wilt. But if I can withhold from cutting them until they're just past their peak, I know that I can get months of joy from their beautifully colored dried flower heads.

ABOVE: One of my 'Limelight' hydrangeas takes home the best-in-show award at the Dutchess County Fair, an annual countywide exhibition of agricultural pursuits and competitions. **OPPOSITE**: The same variety flanks a garden bench and antique fox sculpture near the dovecote. **FOLLOWING PAGES, LEFT**: Climbing hydrangeas make their way up the chimney, with more 'Annabelle' planted below. **FOLLOWING PAGES, RIGHT**: 'Snow Queen' oakleaf hydrangeas are a double-blossom variety with large, lacy flower heads.

BEST IN SHOW

A highlight of my summer is the Dutchess County Fair. It's a local agricultural exposition in nearby Rhinebeck that has been going strong for 170 years, and it draws visitors from around the region and the entire state. More than half a million people attend every year. All-American roller-coaster rides, carnival games, and classic fair food—hello, funnel cakes, corn dogs, and cotton candy—have kept families entertained for generations. Admittedly, I also come for the competitions. I don't have cattle or horses to show, but my flower specimens seem to make the cut year after year (no pun intended). My entries in the poultry fields have also claimed top spots in multiple categories. Although it's more about participating than it is about competing for me, personally, friends will attest that I have never turned down a blue ribbon! Year after year at the fair, as times change and priorities shift, fewer and fewer entrants are being shown across all categories. I primarily exhibit there in hopes of simply inspiring others to try something new.

For the hydrangea and dahlia competitions,

I spend very little time on the preparations. I cut the best of what's in bloom the night before heading to the fair or early that morning, arriving by 7:00 A.M. At 8:15 A.M., the judges do their diligence: Is the foliage damaged? Do the blooms adhere to the stems? By 9:30 A.M., the doors are flung open and throngs of visitors flock to the displays for the big reveal of the year's winners. My show chickens, however, go through a little more preparation. Three to four weeks ahead of showtime, each chicken receives a bath. This is done in advance so that the natural oils and sheen and luster of their feathers has time to return.

I specialize in Buff Orpingtons. For me, they're magical—and their gentle demeanor, their interactions, their prolific egg-laying, and their colors have fascinated me since I was a kid and raised chicks from an incubator with my family. I usually show six to eight chickens, many of which have won awards over the years. I wouldn't miss being a part of these festive gatherings, as they create a special sense of community that hearkens back to a bygone era and is increasingly rare in our current lives.

ABOVE: My winning flock at the Dutchess County Fair. **OPPOSITE**: I gently wash each of the chickens I enter into competition about three to four weeks ahead of time. This allows enough time for the natural oil to return to the birds' feathers. Here, a Buff Orpington rooster gets washed with a gentle pet shampoo.

RISE AND SHINE

When I am hosting a houseful of guests and planning menus for the weekend, a few things come to mind. I love to host and cook, but even the most enthusiastic home chef needs an occasional reprieve from devising and executing numerous meals for multiple people, some of whom may have dietary restrictions, allergies, or aversions to certain foods. Even if I could accommodate every requirement or whim, restrictions imposed by rural life allow for only so much improvisation. In addition, some guests might like to sleep late, and an early, rise-and-shine farmer's breakfast would be lost on them. My preferred course of action allows for flexibility as the weekend rolls on. I will usually cook a Friday dinner at home, which is followed by an early Saturday lunch in town. Dinner that night is back at home, and Sunday consists of a late brunch—perhaps the most important meal of the weekend—even if it's just for a solitary overnight guest.

My kitchen table was previously owned

by Bunny Mellon, and it is the centerpiece of the space and a natural oasis where guests congregate. My marbleized plates set the foundation for a breakfast tableau, flanked by vintage flatware and plain white napkins with a subtle yet sophisticated scalloped edge. A riotous mix of poppies fills a faux-bois cachepot from my studio. For brunch, I will serve platters of creamy slow-cooked scrambled eggs, velvety French toast, strong coffee, brewed iced tea—I love the scented rose blend from Harney & Sons in nearby Millerton—and locally sourced, nitrate-free bacon. Irish soda bread eventually shows up on the menu at some point, too. My own honey and homemade strawberry-rhubarb jam sweeten the deal. I love having a handful of time-tested, standby recipes—they take the stress out of entertaining—but I'm also not afraid to add something new to my repertoire at a moment's notice if a unique or fresh ingredient strikes me at the farmers' market or a guest has a last-minute request.

ABOVE: I'm up early to pick flowers for the breakfast table. OPPOSITE: Breakfast is served with my Marble collection plates and coffee mugs from my studio, antique silver flatware, and scalloped linen napkins. FOLLOWING PAGES: A centerpiece in one of my faux-bois cachepots features a mix of opium and Shirley poppies in shades of lavender, apricot, deep crimson, and pink. I love the mix of their frilly, fringed, and single blooms. PAGES 90–91: Poppies grown at the farm.

'ANGELA ANN'
SWEET PEA

'LAUREN'S GRAPE'
POPPY

'GWEN'S MIDNIGHT
PLUM' POPPY

'FRENCH FLOUNCE' AND
'SUGAR PLUM' POPPIES

OPIUM POPPIES

PAPAVER
SOMNIFERUM

SHIRLEY POPPY

BLACK ASIATIC LILY

ABOVE: A mix of 'Drama Queen', 'French Flounce', 'Ooh La La', 'Lauren's Grape', 'Cupcake', and 'Sugar Plum' poppies awaits arranging. **OPPOSITE**: After cutting and finding an appropriate vessel for display—poppies look best when showcased in something with a wide mouth—the key to a long-lasting arrangement is to briefly sear the bottom of each stem for about ten seconds after it has been cut. That will give you blooms for about four to six days; otherwise, a milky sap will escape the stem, blocking water intake, and they'll quickly wilt.

Growing Herbs

Only recently did I begin to cultivate a proper herb garden. Raising herbs in pots had worked well for me for a long time, and I do continue to grow a few varieties that way, but I had been searching for an ideal spot to grow them in the ground for quite awhile so I could grow more than pots allow. Inspiration finally struck when my mother gifted me a remarkable Victorian collection of terra-cotta edging in a faux-bois pattern that she procured from a Canadian antiques dealer, and I then acquired another set of charming antique English ceramic stoneware edging. Together, they became the framework to create two new herb beds.

The rope pattern of one set and the gently scalloped edges of the other add just enough pattern and delineate the herb garden without distracting or overpowering. The materials feel appropriate to the history of the house, and their patina adds richness and dimension to the garden. Of course, the various textures and shapes of the herbs and their delicate leaves are the primary canvas, and I love completing the composition with just the right border.

The two beds—one in a diamond pattern, the other in an X shape—now flank the kitchen entry. My partner, landscape architect Anthony Bellomo, designed these complementary layouts, and I like their mismatched charm. The borders also help keep the beds defined, because herbs become leggy or unkempt without regular trimming. Certain herbs (I'm looking at you, mint!) can quickly get out of hand without some sort of barrier, so I've found this configuration to be the best marriage of form and function.

The amount of sunshine on the southeast corner of the house turned out to be pretty perfect for my herb garden. An added bonus: the area is right next to the kitchen door, so a quick garnish is always at hand! Because herbs grow so darn fast, you would now think this little patch had been here forever. I love growing lemon verbena for steeping tea, as well as tarragon and basil for whipping up homemade mayonnaise. Sage and rosemary are always at the ready for a roast chicken or a quick fish dish. And I often cut up chives and parsley and dry them in the sun for later use in myriad dishes whenever inspiration strikes.

OPPOSITE: Having fresh herbs by the kitchen door is ideal for adding last-minute garnishes to meals. My partner, Anthony Bellomo, designed the layout for the plantings. **ABOVE**: Freshly harvested shallots are great for marinades, side dishes, and salad dressings.

ABOVE: A week-old baby peacock belies its future beauty and exuberance. **OPPOSITE, TOP TO BOTTOM**: Peacocks preen as part of their grooming, mating, and protection rituals. These are my Buford Bronze and India Blue peacocks. Throughout the summer months, as they roam the farm, the peafowl lose most of their feathers, only to regrow them again in about seven months. As they age, their plumage gets fuller each year.

AUGUST / SEPTEMBER

Have you ever heard the old expression "the dog days of summer"? August certainly brings the warmest days of the year to Millbrook, and my beloved pups Lyon and Fanny feel extra languid from the heat at this time of year. That gives us humans an excuse to slow down a bit as well and enjoy these last hurrahs of summer. Seemingly overnight, a September cold snap can bring the season to an end, like the flip of a switch. Don't get me wrong, autumn is a most glorious time at Clove Brook, but I'm happy to hang on to these light-filled days and evenings by the pool as long as I can.

At the end of August, I always open my garden to the public for the Garden Conservancy's Open Days tour. More than 200 enthusiasts come to meander through the fields and flower beds, meet my fowl, and smell the roses. It's really an honor to share it with others, from armchair gardeners and dreamers to the avid practitioners whose passion for gardening matches my own.

That said, knowing that a few hundred discerning people are about to descend upon Clove Brook keeps me on my toes—and not just in the days beforehand. It really forces me to think about my plantings from year to year so the experience for visitors and guests isn't always the same. While I don't design my garden for strangers—it's a true passion project for me—I see the joy it can inspire in others, whether it's from a single bloom, a quirky color combination, or the unique texture of a plant's foliage.

Soon after, in September, a slight chill starts to descend upon the valley most evenings. I find the week after Labor Day to be a great time to host a cocktail party for friends. It has become my other annual open house of sorts, because the garden is at its most joyful moment—the dahlias are at their peak, and it's a perfect time to reconnect and hear about everyone's summers.

'Oklahoma Pink' zinnias thrive in the late summer sun. Almost effortless to grow and quite profusive, they are great for cutting for flower arrangements. Each year, I sow a different color of seed, but usually stick to one variety to complement the other plantings. The frilly foliage on the left is a large asparagus plant, which will need to be trimmed after the first frost.

THE POOL HOUSE

The second I moved to Clove Brook Farm—in fact, maybe before I even closed on the property, and long before I had a chance to think about designing a new kitchen or replacing the drafty windows—all of my friends urged me to put in a swimming pool (heated, of course). Fifteen years later, I now know that getting the house and kitchen "done" first was the right course. I have no regrets about waiting to put in the pool, although my visitors are certainly happy to have a cool watering hole to share these days. Some other amenities guests now enjoy are comfortable beds, working bathrooms, air-conditioning, and heating—in addition to the many meals served from a productive kitchen over the years—all of which were missing in the early days.

Naturally, a pool needs a pool house, and mine is the latest structural addition to Clove Brook, the realization of a dream I've held for quite some time. A lot of thought and care went into its design, both in terms of function and aesthetics. I wanted something rooted in classical architecture, but nothing that would be an exact match to my house or the dovecote. The farm needed a dose of whimsy without being silly.

Because reaching the pool requires a short hike up a slight incline, guests needed to be rewarded for making the trek. I wanted to give them an oasis of sorts. I chose to site the pool away from the main house for a couple of reasons. First, it allowed me the opportunity to design another garden room around it that I could create and nurture. Second, because I situated it at the top of a hill on the site of a former riding ring, I don't have to look down on an unsightly covered pool during the six coldest months of the year.

My initial inspiration for the pool house came from the temple of Pan, a neoclassical auxiliary building located at Osterley Park in England. From there, I worked with local craftsmen in Millbrook to put my own spin on it. An antler-clad "temple" at Arundel Castle, also in England, gave me the confidence to create my own retreat that has both a stalwart presence and features fanciful flourishes with naturally shed antlers from fallow deer. Somehow, the two disparate ideas go hand in hand and don't appear incongruous. Inside, creature comforts meet basic needs: I found myself going to the main house to get ice for drinks all the time, so an ice maker was quickly installed and has become the ultimate luxury. A bathroom, changing room, and outdoor shower round out my guests' requirements. On the advice of a friend, I installed a washing machine and dryer on-site to avoid having to lug a mountain of towels all the way to the house and back.

OPPOSITE: The antler-adorned neoclassical pool house, with sweeping views of the hills of the Clove Valley in the distance, is based on buildings from two different historic English country-house estates. The capital of each of the pool house's columns is composed of naturally shed antlers from fallow deer.
ABOVE: The design of the rear of the pool house was treated with as much care as its front facade. Laundry appliances—hidden in cabinetry, at left—and an outdoor shower offer all the comforts of home.

LILIES AT THE TABLE

Lunch at the pool is always a casual affair. The mood is relaxed, and there is no agenda. Whether guests come just for a meal or linger for an afternoon of swimming, everyone agrees that his or her blood pressure drops immediately upon entering this area of the farm. The water in the pool clearly has a lulling effect, as guests instantly put away smartphones, curl up on a chaise with a towel, and dive into a pile of magazines, the latest best seller, or another summer read. Time stands still until hunger strikes, and I've chosen to keep meals relaxed as well. Light fare usually includes some combination of curried chicken salad, sliced tomatoes and mozzarella, or a kale salad with other greens picked straight from the garden. I don't overthink it, and I try not to heat up the kitchen.

For my table's centerpiece, I don't have to travel far. Beds of lilies—more than a dozen varieties, some of which reach eight feet tall—are the perfect foil for my vintage laboratory-glass vases, which I've been collecting for years. I love bringing height to the table, and these cylinders add a sculptural effect without blocking guests' views. Because each lily bloom is so colorful and gorgeous, I don't like to overwhelm or overdo it, so I only need to cut four or five stems to make a big impact. Lilies are surprisingly hearty plants, yet their blooms and tender stamens are so delicate and offer a sensuous touch to the table. Each unfurling petal, whether it be striped, mottled, or a single hue, offers so much detail and variety, begging for a closer examination.

ABOVE: Fragrant 'Gold Band' lilies feature bright yellow stripes down the center of each flower petal. **OPPOSITE**: A wall of orange tiger lilies flanks each end of the pool garden. In the foreground, 'Little Spire' Russian sage is a smaller understory plant that adds contrast with its silvery-gray foliage and lavender-colored flowers. Both thrive in well-drained soil and full sunlight.

OPPOSITE: For added interest, I like to stagger the heights of the lilies in my single-stem arrangements placed in laboratory-glass vessels and beakers. ABOVE: An embroidered Italian place mat evokes a fantasy seascape. The Tiffany & Co. flatware is a vintage bamboo pattern designed by Van Day Truex, one of my design icons, and the contemporary plates with geometric patterns are made by Brooklyn ceramist Nicholas Newcomb. The faux-bois salt cellar is my own design.

The pool and surrounding garden, which I've filled with a collection of lilies, purple Russian sage, myriad David Austin roses, and a hornbeam hedge, is perched on the site of a former riding arena, just a short stroll from the main house. The oval shape of the pool was inspired by one in a photograph of a scrapbook given to me by Albert Hadley. **FOLLOWING PAGES**: Some of the lilies grown on the farm.

'CASA BLANCA'

GOLD BAND

'DIZZY'

'MUSCADET'

'BLACK BEAUTY'

'ZEBA'

'ANASTASIA'

'LEVERN
FRIEMANN'

TIGER

DAHLIAS

As the summer season winds down, people often ask me how I keep up with everything at Clove Brook. Dahlias, a favorite of mine, are a perfect example of elegance and efficiency. I try to order any new bulbs, seeds, and tubers a season before I want them to bloom. As the old adage goes, the early bird gets the worm, and the same is true for unique and unusual plants. When I can't get my dahlia tubers a season ahead of time, I still procure them well in advance: I order them in the winter, and they arrive in March. More than 350 get put into pots and primed for planting in April—again, earlier than most people suggest for my area, but I have had great success thus far. In turn, I have a longer succession of blooms. I also always keep an extra dozen (or more) on hand to replace plants that don't make it—and there are always a few.

I find the seemingly infinite variety of dahlias so beguiling. Some are orchid-shaped, and button- and ball-shaped blooms always delight. The miniature ones are great for mixing into large arrangements; pom-poms add character to every centerpiece. Huge dinner-plate varieties, which are often ten to twelve inches in diameter, give joy to even the most jaded gardener. Dahlias were once the favorites of Victorians, but they fell out of fashion for years. In the last couple of decades, these wondrous flowers have regained the adoring following they deserve.

ABOVE: Towering dahlias command a striking presence in the dovecote garden.
OPPOSITE: A mix of dahlia varieties are combined with purple *verbena bonariensis* and castor leaves to create a kaleidoscopic arrangement. The grouping sits atop a similarly vibrant painted hatbox formerly owned by Sister Parish.

ABOVE: A pale pink 'Cafe au Lait' dahlia is the epitome of grace. **OPPOSITE**: Photographs of similar dahlias taken in the garden were transferred and fired onto ceramic plates of my studio's design. Little garden critters accent the rims. Berry-colored napkins and amethyst goblets echo the palette. My friend Julie "June Bug" Williamson created the recipe for the flatbread. **FOLLOWING PAGES**: A selection of dahlias grown at the farm.

The garden is at its finest hour in late August. Morning dew gives each plant, each leaf, and each petal a lustrous sparkle as the clouds lift and the midday sun emerges. A profusion of dahlias—some six feet tall—seemingly reach for the sky. Flanking the dovecote, six young apple trees have flourished over the past season.

Cocktails in the Garden

My annual end-of-summer cocktail party in the garden arrives every year like clockwork. Just as the days begin to get noticeably shorter after Labor Day and the first nip of autumn arrives, friends know that my yearly get-together is just around the corner. Its spot on the calendar always seems a bit serendipitous, but there is a real rhythm to it—a glorious harvest moon is never far behind. Although it is considerably late in the growing season, in many ways the garden is at its peak at this time. Hundreds of dahlia blooms stand sentinel, towering more than six feet tall. Other blooms are beginning to taper; some foliage is starting to take on just a hint of yellow or red; and a few things are completely spent and left to dry, bringing depth and texture that adds another level of dimension to the garden.

A start time of 6:30 P.M. ensures that guests will still have a good hour of daylight for touring the gardens before darkness falls. The soft glow at that time of day, punctuated by the warm flickering light coming from the countless candles scattered about, makes it a picture-perfect time for taking photographs— no filter required! If we're lucky, a spectacular sunset is the icing on the cake, or, perhaps, the perfect amuse-bouche before guests move inside for dinner. Even though this evening is a regular event on my personal social calendar, each year I'm still somehow surprised to realize that hosting a fete for 100 people is quite an undertaking! Accordingly, I find that once again, a simple plan keeps things moving swimmingly and allows me to retain a hands-on approach to hosting without engaging an army of outside help.

I always compose the flower arrangements a day or two ahead of time. The same goes for my salad dressings, perfect for letting the flavors meld. I purchase everything for the bar three weeks before the event; by now, I know that I'll need two cases of white and red wines and ninety-eight bottles of various mixers. Yes, exactly ninety-eight. The first time I held my party, I never guessed how many bottles of sparkling water I'd go through. I've never forgotten, and I have yet to run out ever again! The more often one entertains, the more confident one becomes: we learn what works and what to let go of. Even when something doesn't work, it's not a defeat—just another opportunity to learn, adjust, revise, and move on. Another key to success is keeping the fare simple. The food I serve is, if I do say so myself, as good as anything a caterer might prepare, and my guests clearly love it. Simple stews, four different green salads, a variety of comfort foods—think meatloaf and lobster rolls—along with corn on the cob, celery remoulade, and store-bought Heath bar cakes and key lime pies for dessert make for the perfect repast.

OPPOSITE: Party prep. Serendipity, one of my favorite fabrics by Sister Parish, covers a banquet table that's being set up to serve drinks and hors d'oeuvres at my annual autumn open house for friends. In the meantime, a profusion of dinner-plate dahlias anchors the setting. **FOLLOWING PAGES**: Guests congregate on the terrace and in the dovecote garden and wander up to the pool house—a few venture into the chicken coops! **PAGES 122–23**: A collection of dahlias grown at the farm.

'HOLLY HUSTON'

'PURPLE TAIHEIJO'

'BEN HUSTON'

DAHLIA SORENSENII

'BASHFUL'

'TAIHEIYO'

'TARTAN'

'VERRONE'S OBSIDIAN'

'FERNCLIFF INSPIRATION'

'DRUMMER BOY'

'AC PAINT'

'PAUL SMITH'

'LIGHTS OUT'

'KARMA PROSPERO'

'ROSY WINGS'

'MISTY IMAGINATION'

'CHAT NOIR'

'PENHILL DARK MONARCH'

'WALTER HARDISTY'

'BROOKSIDE SNOWBALL'

'LABYRINTH'

'HONKA WHITE'

'VASSIO MEGGOS'

'MAARN'

'BREAK OUT'

'FAIRWAY SPUR'

'VERA SEYFANG'

'CHILSON'S PRIDE'

'JUST MARRIED'

CHOOSING A VASE

Selecting a vase is a remarkably personal task. Showcasing flowers in simple, clear vases is the de facto route for many of us, and admittedly, it's difficult to go wrong that way; however, I believe that different flowers, occasions, and settings call for different vessels. Marrying the right blooms with the perfect vase creates a more compelling overall composition, similar to the manner in which a perfect picture frame can elevate a painting or photograph. I have amassed countless vases, cachepots, bottles, bowls, and urns over the years in a variety of colors and finishes. I display them together so I can grab one in a hurry and get fresh-cut stems submerged in water as soon as possible. Even when they're not in use, I love seeing the light reflecting off of them and the pleasing pattern of their curved shapes, scalloped edges, and other decorative flourishes.

Some of my pots are Victorian, others are midcentury; a handful are truly special, while others are thrift-store finds that have no particular provenance but make me happy. I keep a handful of my own designs on hand as well. If you don't have the space to hold countless vases for every possible flower-arranging scenario that might present itself, don't fret! Just make sure you have a small, medium, and large option. In a pinch, low glass tumblers or tall everyday pitchers will suffice, and they often look like a million bucks. Whatever you are arranging, sharp clippers for cutting stems will save you time, and fresh water every few days will make your design last exponentially longer.

ABOVE, FROM LEFT: A stem of Zeba lilies in an amethyst bottle. Orange and red ranunculus reside in an amber vase. A Beallara Ysabella 'Lunar Eclipse' orchid in one of my studio's faux-bois cachepots.
OPPOSITE: Colored glass, clear glass, white bisque porcelain, and tinted ceramics—a cornucopia of vessels awaits flowers. Simple and sculptural, ornate and elegant, there's a vase for every occasion.

Summer Calendar

JUNE

Peonies are at their peak the first week, prime for cutting and arranging.

Move four-week-old baby chicks to their new coops in the barn.

Host alfresco lunches and dinners for friends.

Trim boxwood and hornbeam, and spray boxwood with anti-blight fertilizer.

Mulch flower beds again; heavy mulching deters weeds.

Fertilize and spray houseplants with horticultural oil and insecticidal soap to control indoor pests and insects.

Harvest Russian kale and snap peas.

Create arrangements using sweet-pea flowers at the end of the month.

JULY

Celebrate the Fourth of July with a late lunch or dinner and fireworks. Hang the cotton bunting!

Order lily bulbs for fall.

Make lemon verbena tea.

Sleep with the windows open and enjoy the cool night air.

Collect allium heads to dry for Christmas decorations.

Wash and clean chickens in anticipation of competition and judging at next month's Dutchess County Fair.

Apply last fertilization to roses for the season.

AUGUST

Create flower arrangements using dahlias. Don't be afraid to cut a generous amount of the stem—it encourages more growth and blooms.

Early in the month, order provisions for the end-of-summer garden party to be held after Labor Day.

Enter chickens and hydrangeas into juried competitions at the Dutchess County Fair.

Gather fallen branches and other garden debris and have a bonfire with s'mores and drinks.

Stock the pantry with an assortment of iced teas, cheeses, chips, sesame crackers, sodas, beer and wine for languorous afternoons by the pool.

Deadhead spent flower blooms, including cosmos, zinnias, and dahlias.

Remove seedpods from lilies and peonies after they've finished flowering.

GIFT OF THE SEASON

Friends' eyes light up when they receive a carton of colorful farm-fresh eggs laid by my Araucana, Buff Orpington, and Copper Marans chickens. Their respective blue, cream, and dark brown hues make for a delightful dozen.

SUMMER RECIPES

CARAMELIZED PAN-ROASTED SHALLOTS

Serves 6

This recipe is a variation of one I learned from my friend and cooking teacher, Mimi Thorisson.

12 large shallots

3 Tbsp. duck fat

2 tsp. fine sea salt

1 Tbsp. turbinado or granulated sugar

1. Preheat oven to 450°F.

2. Cut shallots in half vertically, leaving the skin on.

3. Heat a large cast-iron roasting pan or two cast-iron skillets over medium-high heat. Melt the duck fat in the hot pan, then evenly sprinkle with the salt and sugar.

4. Place shallots in the pan cut-side down. Then immediately transfer the pan or skillets to the preheated oven.

5. Check shallots for doneness after 20 minutes by lifting one. The cut side should be caramelized and dark brown in color when done.

6. Serve hot with steak, chicken, or salmon—these shallots really go with everything!

PERFECT SCRAMBLED EGGS

Serves 2

I learned this recipe from French chef Paul Laboulais in St. Barts.

Coconut oil or nonstick cooking spray

6 large eggs

2 pinches salt

Freshly ground black pepper, to taste

2 tsp. Dijon mustard (optional)

2 oz. cheddar or Gruyère cheese, grated (optional)

½ cup grated zucchini (optional)

2 Tbsp. chopped fresh herbs (optional)

1 avocado, diced (optional)

1. Coat a heavy-bottomed stainless steel pan with coconut oil.

2. Break eggs into pan, and add salt and pepper to taste. Turn heat to medium high.

3. Whisk eggs together, without stopping, for about 3 minutes. The eggs will slowly begin to curdle. Be sure no eggs are sticking to the bottom.

4. When eggs are almost done, but still wet, turn heat off and continue to whisk. Add any optional ingredients, if using. The eggs will finish cooking from residual heat in the pan.

FALL

OCTOBER

The first frost at Clove Brook comes around October 15. While you'd think that would create some dormancy around the farm, it's still a surprisingly active time, both inside and out. All of the storm windows are pulled from the barn and cleaned, ready to replace the screens I've had in all summer. Around the same time, my carpenter drops off the first delivery of four cords of wood for the winter. He neatly stacks it on the porch near the garage to keep it dry and close at hand so we don't have to go stomping through the snow on a frigid night. Four cords seems like a lot of wood to many people, but when I'm home, the fireplace in the kitchen burns all day, and everyone loves to gather there. If there were ever any question whether autumn has arrived, gourds, picture-perfect pumpkins, and dried corn in decorative arrangements and wreaths signal that change is in the air. In the dovecote, each of my fowl is wormed. The birds are adept at handling cold temperatures, but the dovecote is kept warm and tight so they can avoid drafts, which can be dangerous to them.

Back outside, with the lawn and surrounding fields, I can tell you that I'm not one for raking leaves. A mower mulches them back into the ground, and once they've stopped falling, we don't cut the grass again until spring. After the mulching is completed, all of the farm's tractors, tillers, and tools are serviced and stowed away as well. Following the first frost, it takes about two weeks to dig up, sort, and store all of my 400-plus dahlia tubers (they multiply once they're planted). They're put into crates filled with wood shavings for safekeeping until it's time to replant them in mid-April. Once the tubers are up and the dovecote garden has been cleaned and tilled, a barrage of other bulbs go in for spring: tulips, narcissi, lilies, snowdrops, crocuses, and more. In all, about 8,000 new bulbs get planted over the course of a few weeks.

PREVIOUS PAGES: A centuries-old maple tree casts a long shadow over the grounds. Its fall foliage changes from green to yellow and orange, then to a fiery red and burgundy. **OPPOSITE**: Hanging out with two of my Buff Orpington chickens, a breed that can lay more than 200 eggs a year.

ABOVE: My chickens and turkeys are allowed to freely roam the farm anytime I am at the property and can keep an eye on them. **OPPOSITE**: A Buff Orpington rooster (center) mingles with black-and-white Light Sussex roosters and gray Blue Slate turkeys.

ABOVE: Dried calico corn is wrapped with a purple and white–striped ribbon that I recycled from a gift I received from my mother (which, in fact, was from another present I had given her!). I always suggest buying quality ribbon, as it can be used again and again. **OPPOSITE**: Every year, I adapt a four-tiered plant stand to create a striking arrangement of heirloom pumpkins and gourds, each featuring unique colors, textures, and patterns. Showing a range of sizes—from teeny-tiny to gigantic—creates a dazzling display.

COLLECTING

Collecting is very important to me. It's more than a pastime; it's like an obsession for me to stumble upon an object, particularly an antique or vintage item, take interest in it, and learn all that I can about it. My front hall, which is the former entrance that everyone used to come through, contains a disparate, unmatched mix of things that speak to me. While just a pass-through, it's a major artery to all parts of the house—it connects the two main downstairs living spaces with the private quarters upstairs.

I find it refreshing to have things you love on display whenever you can, including in rooms where you don't really linger. Even when I'm running through the hall to sign for a delivery or answer the phone, I always get a smile on my face because every single piece has a significant meaning. In the adjacent living room, one of my most recent acquisitions is also one of the most personal. The renowned interior designer Mario Buatta was a close friend, and he lived not far from my apartment in New York City. After his death, I was able to procure a series of his fabled spaniel paintings, which meant so much to him. To honor his legacy, I took his cue and displayed them in a similar way to how he had them hanging in his famous living room. I wasn't looking to imitate his style; I wanted to create a moment in which he would hopefully nod in approval. The lesson I've learned over the years is to buy what you love, and it will always, eventually, find a perfect place in your home.

ABOVE: The best homes are filled with things that have a special meaning, regardless of provenance or price tag. My foyer holds so many cherished pieces. My friend, the artist Clare Potter, is famous for her ceramic designs of flowers, flower arrangements, and fruits and vegetables. For me, she created a porcelain composition featuring Japanese anemones, as well as ceramic eggs based on the colors of those laid by my chickens at the farm. **OPPOSITE**: I'm always inspired by the work of iconic interior designers. A gilt tole dog's head was once owned by Mario Buatta, and I cherish the framed watercolor by Mark Hampton of Albert Hadley's former barn in Maine. The wallpaper is by Cole & Son.

This collection of eighteenth-
and nineteenth-century spaniel
and other dog portraits was
formerly owned by Buatta.
As an homage, I recently
arranged them on my walls in
a manner similar to how they
were displayed in his iconic
living room, complete with
blue satin ribbons that were
one of his signature flourishes.
The portraits on the left are
of my ancestors, Hosea and
Harriet Goodell, and they seem
to enjoy the new company.

ABOVE: The antique Bavarian hall tree in the foyer, adorned with tinsel garland, was previously owned by Albert Hadley. He had the foresight to give this large, foreboding piece of dark wood furniture a coat of white paint, which transformed it into something jolly. **OPPOSITE**: Animals play a huge part in my life—even inanimate ones. Each figure features a joyful countenance.

POTTED PLANTS

Throughout the house and garden, I often put together other sorts of collections, although they're with living things, not inanimate objects, and the need is primarily born out of necessity more than desire. As the year and growing season roll on, it never fails that I end up with a magpie assortment of plants in individual pots and containers scattered about the property. Some are extra seedlings that never found a place in the ground; others are fledgling cuttings that I'm trying nurture. On occasion, it's a sick plant that I try to nurse back to health. To make sense of the chaos, and to bring some efficiency to watering and feeding, I will put together little groupings and place them atop a table, on a shelf, on a pedestal, or even on a rolling cart. My rule of thumb is to bring a point of consistency to each assemblage. You can focus on plants with similar foliage or colored blooms, or just mix a variety of disparate plants together, making sure they are in matching or coordinating pots. Regarding the latter, herbs and annuals and succulents can all mingle yet not look out of place when grouped in complementary containers. Having one common thread reduces all of the cacophony, and the same advice holds true for plants originally potted with purpose. In both instances, the end result is a pretty display where the whole is greater than the sum of its parts.

ABOVE, FROM LEFT: A stately conical planter by Pennoyer Newman is made of a composite of pummeled marble, rock, and resin, so it's surprisingly lightweight. An ornate antique terra-cotta urn provides a focal point in the dining room. A cast iron urn with antlers holds a sculptural Pencil cactus. OPPOSITE: A painted antique plant stand provides an opportunity to create harmony out of a cacophonous group of mismatched plants that rotates regularly.

142

APPLE HARVEST

One of the joys of living in the Hudson Valley is being a part of the agricultural community here. Apple orchards have always played a significant role in the region's rich history, and you can still find them dotting the area's rolling hills. When I bought Clove Brook, there were two mature Macoun apple trees and two McIntosh apple trees on the property that provided me a framework to imagine my own orchard. I buy most of my heirloom trees from a well-respected grower, Trees of Antiquity. For the most part, if you're looking to grow an old variety of apple, you'll be limited to procuring saplings that are only about thirty inches tall. The rarer the variety, the less chance you'll find a large tree, unless it's from a decommissioned orchard. Thankfully, apple trees aren't the slowest growers (they're not the fastest, either), and you can certainly mark their progress year after year.

When it comes to harvesting apples, I've found that I get a bumper crop every other season. Besides the trees' reliable blossoms every May, always around the time of the Kentucky Derby, much of what determines a successful crop is left to the whims of nature, and I just go with the flow. Bramley's Seedling, Cox's Orange Pippin, and Esopus Spitzenburg are my preferred types for baking tarts and juicing, and I now have fourteen trees. I also acquired an old-fashioned apple press and believe that the best cider comes from blending a mix of varieties, from sweet to tart. Making cider has become an annual tradition, and friends are shocked by how much fruit it takes to get one single glass of juice. Two bushels often yield just about a half gallon. After cranking the press by hand, the resulting juice is considered liquid gold, but it's worth the effort: nothing store-bought can compare.

ABOVE: Ripe Macoun apples are a staple in my fall recipes. **OPPOSITE**: A wheelbarrow full of McIntosh apples is ready for the cider press. Before the first hard frost, I have to remove as many as possible from the trees so the crop isn't ruined by the freezing temperatures. Once they're picked, I can store them in the barn for a couple of weeks before they need to be processed.

ABOVE: Portable and lightweight, tripod ladders are specifically designed for orchard harvesting, such as with this apple tree. **OPPOSITE, CLOCKWISE FROM TOP LEFT**: A bushel of McIntosh apples is sorted, and any that have major bruising or other flaws are put into the compost. With a manual press, juice extraction is a hands-on endeavor. It sometimes requires three or four apples just to get one eight-ounce glass of juice! My friend Ashley's son, Andrew, feeds the cast-iron grinding box while I crank. Once the apples are ground, the remaining pulp is pressed for juice.

OPPOSITE, CLOCKWISE FROM TOP LEFT: My apple tart is a crowd-pleaser and easy to make; a simple store-bought puff pastry is rolled out. Slices of apples are coated in raw sugar and cinnamon. A glaze of apricot jam is the last touch after baking. Placing each slice in parallel lines creates a striking presentation. **ABOVE**: The happy result.

ANIMAL ATTRACTION

By now you've seen that when I entertain outside, I love to take a bit of the indoors with me, as alfresco dining doesn't have to be relegated to melamine plates and paper napkins. While you won't find me toting the sofa out onto the lawn, I don't see any reason that interior objects can't be reassembled en plein air to create a fun tableau under the sky and stars. For an autumn luncheon in the orchard, I love to bring together some of my favorite decorative critters. Filled with late-blooming Japanese anemones, a pair of Staffordshire dog spill vases—flanking a giant artichoke sculpture of my design—serve as centerpieces but are just one part of the menagerie I've assembled. The dinner plates, a collaboration between my pottery studio and the artist Cathy Graham, are adorned with an array of painted bunnies, birds, squirrels, butterflies, and grasshoppers. They're so charming, and guests love to examine them and discover all of the tiny little details that Cathy incorporates into her cheerful designs, such as currants, shells, and feathers. Venetian glass honeybees are scattered around the table atop a vintage blue-and-white tattersall cloth and are a subtle reference to my real-life bees and their nearby hives. At last, my antique wolf sculpture—not one to be left out of the festivities—keeps a watch over all of us from atop his fieldstone base at the end of the orchard allée. The subtle assemblage of animal motifs, natural elements, and interior accessories brings a smile to everyone's faces and adds a welcome touch of whimsy and humor to the table while retaining an air of easy elegance.

ABOVE: Arranged in Staffordshire vases, wispy 'Honorine Jobert' and 'Ruffled Swan' Japanese anemone flowers seemingly dance when they catch an autumn breeze. **OPPOSITE**: A tattersall cloth with crisp lines balances out the tablescape's more decorative flourishes, such as Venetian-glass insects and horn flatware. My friend, the artist and illustrator Cathy Graham, and I collaborated on the dinner plates, which feature an assortment of whimsical wildlife designs. The monogrammed napkins are by Madison Monograms. **FOLLOWING PAGES**: A ceramic artichoke of my design serves as the centerpiece alongside a pair of Staffordshire dog vases overflowing with Japanese anemones.

ABOVE: A lacy, fall-blooming clematis envelops the paddock fence. **OPPOSITE**: I constructed a fieldstone base to showcase my antique cast-iron wolf, which was designed by French artist Henri Alfred Jacquemart. The sculpture previously resided at Doris Duke's estate in New Jersey; at Clove Brook, its life-size stature is a formidable presence.

ABOVE: With an airtight seal, honey I've harvested can last indefinitely. Beekeeping is a pastime that I enjoy, but the benefits that the bees' pollination bring to the garden can't be understated. **OPPOSITE, CLOCKWISE FROM TOP LEFT**: In a layer of protective gear, I open the hive to remove the bees. A honey-laden frame is ready to be processed. When it's time for bottling, the honey is a beautiful amber hue. I use a fork to uncap the honeycombs before placing the frames into the extractor, which spins at a high velocity to release the liquid.

NOVEMBER

A t Thanksgiving, the past, present, and future all come together in my cozy dining room. Every year, the holiday is a shared experience. I rotate hosting with a few other couples. When it's my turn, I'm reminded of the gratitude I have for their company and longtime friendship, plus the unfiltered joy and excitement I see in their children's eyes at the first sight of a giant turkey and all of the desserts. Even when I glance at the chandelier, a design by my dear friend, the late Albert Hadley, I am gently reminded of the mentorship and counsel he provided me. It's a full-circle moment that I cherish each time.

And while the season is about celebrating traditions, I take a bit of an unorthodox approach to the tablescape decor and forge ahead with making new memories each year. My friends Bunny Williams and John Rosselli set a high bar for table settings, from which I draw inspiration. They've also championed serving meals buffet-style, so that people can pick and choose what they want to eat. I've adopted the same approach over the years.

At a recent Thanksgiving, I created an autumnal feeling without the usual suspects. Gourds, pumpkins, and dried corn are easy to source and easy to use, but I chose to relegate them to the outdoor decor, which has its own festive spirit. Instead, I took my cue from a palette of rich, vibrant jewel-tone colors to create a mood that was both cozy and chic. Everyday chrysanthemums stood out for their unexpected amethyst color and were mixed among vases and pots of black 'Witchcraft' orchids, blue thistles, and chocolate cosmos.

But as with any fresh take on tradition that I employ, the season always comes back to family and friends. Handcrafted and hand-painted ceramic fruits and vegetables by my friend, artist Clare Potter, adorn the cloth like a deconstructed cornucopia. My godmother's silver Tiffany julep cups are a testament to using antiques in new ways, and their deployment on this special day is something she would no doubt consider worthy of a toast. Cheers!

OPPOSITE: My Marble collection of dinnerware in brown and white anchors each Thanksgiving place setting atop a tablecloth created from my favorite Brunschwig & Fils Le Lac fabric. The jewel-toned palette echoes the colors of the miniature ceramic fruits, nuts, and vegetables, designed by ceramist Clare Potter, scattered across the table. The chicken accent piece was once owned by the Duchess of Devonshire.

DRYING HYDRANGEAS

By now, you know how much I love hydrangeas and how much their blooms add to the landscape with little effort. I extend their usefulness by drying the blooms in the autumn. They are a gift that keeps on giving well beyond the growing season. Few other flowering plants promise as much. Cut back the hydrangeas when their heads start to turn pink. The color shift is subtle at first, but it's unmistakable. Since most of my plants are mature, they're large. So when I cut, I try to leave a thirty-inch stem on the blooms so that I have different options for arranging them later. People are sometimes surprised by how much I prune my hydrangeas, but it stimulates growth in the next season. After stripping all of the leaves off of the branches, I start by creating a giant arrangement in one of my favorite urns in the living room. Thankfully the stems no longer need water, but they do need help staying in position, so you can use chicken wire to create a cone shape to place in the urn. The spaces between the wires are perfect for holding each stem in place, and it makes for a stable anchor. From there, it's just a matter of adding the stems and attempting to get them to reach as far as the ceiling. I might execute one or two small arrangements with the remainder, but I also give big bunches of dried hydrangeas to friends who love to display them as much as I do. They can last forever in a dry spot. Keeping them dust-free is often the biggest challenge!

PREVIOUS PAGES: Instead of a solitary centerpiece, arrangements run the length of the table, which is surrounded by my beloved dining chairs in the style of Frances Elkins. Potted black 'Witchcraft' orchids fill the middle spot, and an assortment of colored bud vases filled with purple chrysanthemums, spiky blue thistles, and chocolate cosmos stretch from end to end. The dark hues of the flowers are reflected in the amethyst goblets and similarly colored monogrammed linens. **ABOVE**: 'Limelight' hydrangea. **OPPOSITE**: A sugar maple is ablaze with glorious fall colors. The 'Limelight' hydrangeas along the fencerow are ideal for drying this time of year. **FOLLOWING PAGES, LEFT, CLOCKWISE FROM TOP LEFT**: I retain as much of the hydrangea stem as possible when I cut them. Once most of the leaves have been removed, I carry big bundles into the house for arranging. The flowers are placed in the vase one at a time. I start at the bottom of the urn's edge and pile them as high as I can go. **FOLLOWING PAGES, RIGHT**: The large flower heads of the 'Limelight' hydrangea turn a beautiful shade of dusty pink.

SEED COLLECTING

While seed collection and organization might not seem like the most glamorous part of farm life, it is an oddly gratifying chore because I know it will yield huge results next summer. Most gardeners who start plants from seed purchase them from a catalog, at their local nursery, or at the garden center of a big-box retailer. I do all of those things too for tried-and-true basics that can't be improved on or when I know it's not worth spending extra money on certain seeds. But I'm always excited when I'm able to harvest the seeds from existing plants in the garden. As flowers have cross-pollinated throughout the year, you may find yourself with some unexpected flower colors or striped markings that you never could have imagined—and this is your chance to

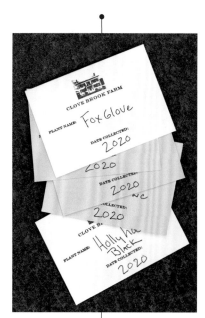

save their seeds. Seed retrieval is easy: cut any dried flower heads or pods once they've faded and simply shake out the seeds onto a clean counter surface or a sheet of paper.

Then, store the seeds in simple brown paper bags or envelopes in a dry spot with little humidity. For me, that's a drawer in my basement. If I have a good year, I give extras away as gifts (there's usually no shortage of seeds). It's quite cost-effective as well—buying lots of new packets every year adds up quickly.

Good plants to try collecting from include lupines, hollyhocks, nicotianas, foxgloves, columbines, castor beans, and sunflowers. But don't waste your time with sweet peas—the seeds are notoriously difficult to retrieve from the spent plant, so I just purchase those anew every year.

ABOVE: I love to give packets of seeds gathered at the farm as gifts to friends, especially when I know someone has a favorite flower. **OPPOSITE**: Poppy, nicotiana, lupine, and hollyhock seeds get sorted at season's end. Gathering them now is not only cost-effective—I also know they will yield special results. Certain plants have been cross-pollinated throughout the season, so I'm able to gather seeds with one-of-a-kind color and petal variations that simply can't be store-bought.

ABOVE: Just as the roof was placed on my new garage, my friend Stephen Sills suggested I should have built a greenhouse instead. I think he was right! Nonetheless, I have created an environment in the space that's conducive to overwintering my plants. Most importantly, growing lights are specially calibrated to mimic the sun's light and are placed on timers that are kept in sync with the season **OPPOSITE**: Most of my plants are grouped by height. Short plants, such as agaves, flank the perimeter, while tall plants, such as gardenias, palms, citrus, and alocasias, reside in the middle. There are movable racks for starting and growing seedlings, as well as an area for potting.

PLANTING BULBS

Planting bulbs can be intimidating for a novice. Figuring out the hole depth and spacing can be daunting the first time you do it. Thanks to the bulbs' appearance, you might not even know which side of the bulb is the top. Don't fret! Most growers provide explicit planting instructions that are usually foolproof. The primary thing to remember is that bulbs need what's called a "chilling period" in order to successfully bloom in the spring— cold temperatures stimulate a biochemical response that initiates root growth and flower formation. On average, that's about twelve to sixteen weeks. I order most of my bulbs to arrive around October 15. Growers usually ship them according to when it's time to plant them in your area. Lily bulbs, for instance, need to go into the ground as soon as they arrive by mail.

There's a little more time with tulips, but don't hold off too long or the weeks will go by and suddenly they won't have enough of a chilling period in the ground.

A pickax is essential in helping to break up the rocky soil that I have at the farm. Dibbers are handy for planting small bulbs, such as crocuses, snowdrops, and *Muscari*. They are also ideal for planting things in a random pattern in clumps, as opposed to big beds of bulbs. A standard-sized shovel works for creating those large troughs for when I'm doing mass plantings of tulips and fritillarias, and a drill outfitted with an auger (which is like a really large bit) lets me plant bulbs one at a time. It's a great, efficient tool for helping create a natural look. Plus, it helps get bulbs into tight spaces where a large shovel might damage the roots of nearby trees and other plants.

ABOVE, FROM LEFT: I use a drill with an auger bit to plant an individual lily bulb. Large trenches are dug for mass plantings of white fritillaria and tulips. The bulbs are watered after being covered with a layer of topsoil.
OPPOSITE: My garden essentials include, from left, rubber gloves (for dry hands), a flat pitchfork (for lifting dahlia tubers), a spade (for digging little trenches), auger bits (for drilling and planting individual bulbs), dibbers (for planting large seeds), a pickaxe (for unlodging rocky soil), and a long-handled plugger (for bulb planting, weeding, and soil testing).

LILIUM
SUPERBUM

'BLACK
BEAUTY' LILY

ALLIUM

ALLIUM

'LEVERN FRIEMANN' LILY

GARLIC

SCILLA

SNOWDROP

CROCUS

CROCUS

TULIP

TULIP

SNOWFLAKE

HYACINTH

NARCISSUS

FRITILLARIA

NARCISSUS

RELEASING THE DOVES

Throughout the year, but more so in the fall, I release my doves into the wild. They have fine accommodations in the dovecote, but I joke that it's an opportunity for them to stretch their legs a bit, so to speak, and to some degree it is. I've always been fascinated by their remarkable homing instincts and their ability to fly back to their nests from wherever they're released, no training required. One of the only downsides to this practice is that there are predators, such as large hawks, that prey on them.

To prepare, I gather a dozen or so of my birds into an old wooden crate that was built specifically to transport poultry. Taking them to a nearby field, I release them one at

a time. After flying around a bit, they get their bearings and start to make their way home for nourishment within hours. Scientists believe the earth's magnetic field guides them—the birds have a built-in compass, although the exact science behind their abilities is still somewhat of a mystery. Back at Clove Brook, the dovecote features a small door that opens in one direction, allowing the birds to return to their habitat with ease while also restricting other doves from escaping. If you've never seen homing birds in action, I certainly urge you to find an aviary exhibition or showcase. There are even sporting clubs with pigeon-racing events! Their navigational abilities will astound you.

PREVIOUS PAGES: Flowering bulbs prefer to be stored in cool, dark, and dry places and should not be overcrowded. ABOVE: A white pigeon perches outside a nesting box in the dovecote. OPPOSITE: From time to time, I transfer my pigeons to a nearby field and release them so they can exercise. After flying around for half an hour or so, their homing abilities—a trait of the breed—instinctually guide them back to the dovecote on the farm. Longtime pigeon keepers have a list of best practices to ensure the birds' safety in the wild. (Birds kept indoors as domesticated pets should never be released outside at any time.)

FALL CALENDAR

SEPTEMBER

Celebrate the end of another summer with a cocktail party in the garden around Labor Day.

Harvest honey.

Trim boxwood and hornbeam, and spray boxwood with anti-blight fertilizer.

Celebrate my birthday.

Search online for upcoming antiques auctions—fall is a great time to hunt for one-of-a-kind treasures.

Pick apples later in the month.

Make tarts, pies, applesauce, and cider.

Research mail-order seed catalogs so that orders can be placed before vendors run out of any limited stock.

OCTOBER

Cover pool after Columbus Day weekend.

Move all citrus and tropical plants into the heated garage.

Dig up dahlia tubers ten days after the last frost.

Plant tulips, lilies, snowdrops, daffodils, and allium bulbs outside for next year.

Start refrigerated cooling of hyacinth bulbs for blooms in January.

Order Christmas cards.

Welcome visitors to the farm for the Garden Conservancy's Open Days garden tour.

Collect and dry seeds.

Clear beds of dead plants.

Plant the first round of paperwhites one month ahead of Thanksgiving for blooms by that holiday.

Pot and water amaryllis for December blooms.

NOVEMBER

Start planning for Thanksgiving meals at the beginning of the month.

Prune white hydrangeas, excluding oak-leaf and blue varieties.

Trim lily stems. Leave them

long after blooming, so they will grow even taller next year.

Put a fresh layer of chicken or cow manure over the flower and vegetable beds.

Wrap burlap around the Chinese juniper plants to protect them from frost and wind.

Create a Thanksgiving menu and a list of what can be done ahead of time, including shopping and polishing silver.

Plant last bulbs the weekend after Thanksgiving before the ground freezes.

GIFT OF THE SEASON

People can't believe the taste difference between store-bought apple cider and fresh hand-pressed cider from the farm, which doesn't have preservatives or additives. A carton of it is a quintessentially autumnal gift.

FALL RECIPES

CHEESE-AND-HERB SOUFFLÉS
Serves 6

Gail Monaghan, my friend and cooking teacher, introduced this process to me. I've tinkered with the ingredients a bit.

6 12 oz. charlotte molds or ramekins

6 Tbsp. salted butter, softened, plus more for greasing molds

½ cup plus 6 Tbsp. grated Parmesan cheese, divided

10 large egg whites

1 tsp. cream of tartar

1½ tsp. fine sea salt, divided

1 clove garlic, minced

6 Tbsp. all-purpose flour

2 cups whole milk

¼ tsp. cayenne

¼ tsp. freshly grated nutmeg

¼ tsp. freshly ground black pepper

6 large egg yolks

6 Tbsp. grated Gruyère cheese

¼ cup chopped mixed fresh herbs, such as chives, parsley, and basil

1. Preheat oven to 400°F.

2. Butter six charlotte molds and coat with ½ cup grated Parmesan cheese. Place molds on a baking sheet lined with parchment paper.

3. Mix remaining grated Parmesan with Gruyère and set aside.

4. Add egg whites, cream of tartar, and ½ tsp. salt to the bowl of a stand mixer fitted with a whisk attachment, then whisk on low. Raise the speed every few minutes until you reach the highest speed. Continue to whisk until soft peaks form, about 5 to 10 minutes.

5. Melt 6 Tbsp. butter in a heavy-bottomed saucepan, add the garlic, and cook for 1 minute. Whisk in flour and stir constantly until golden, about 2 to 3 minutes.

6. Add milk to the saucepan and whisk vigorously. Add cayenne, nutmeg, remaining salt, and pepper. Bring to a boil while continually whisking. Continue to whisk for 3 to 5 minutes, or until sauce is very thick. Off the heat, whisk in egg yolks one at a time. Add all but 3 Tbsp. of cheese mixture and herbs. Taste for seasoning. (This base can be made up to 3 days ahead and refrigerated. Bring to room temperature and heat over boiling water to tepid before continuing with step 7.)

7. Thoroughly mix ¼ of the beaten egg whites into the base to temper it. Add this mixture to remaining egg whites. Using a spatula, slowly and very gently fold mixture into egg whites. (The soufflés won't rise if you deflate the whites.) It's fine if some small clumps of egg white don't fully incorporate.

8. Fill molds to just over the lip and sprinkle with reserved cheese.

9. Place inside preheated oven and reduce heat to 375°F. Bake for 20 minutes, or until the tops are browned and the soufflés have set. Serve immediately—a soufflé waits for no one!

APPLE TART
Serves 6

1 frozen puff pastry, defrosted

3 Granny Smith or other tart apples

¼ cup plus 2 Tbsp. turbinado sugar, divided

1 tsp. ground cinnamon

3 Tbsp. salted butter, cut into small pieces

¼ cup peach jam

2 Tbsp. Calvados

1. Preheat oven to 400°F.

2. Roll out puff pastry into a 9-by-13-inch rectangle and place on a parchment-lined baking sheet.

3. Leaving the skin on, core apples and cut into ¼-inch wedges.

4. In a medium bowl, mix together cinnamon and ¼ cup sugar. Add apple wedges and toss to coat.

5. Arrange apple wedges in tight rows on pastry sheet, leaving a 1-inch border on all sides. Sprinkle slices with remaining sugar and pieces of butter.

6. Bake in the center of the oven for about 40 minutes, or until tart is nicely browned and crust is cooked through.

7. While tart is baking, heat peach jam and Calvados in a small pan until jam is dissolved. Brush glaze on finished tart while still hot.

8. Cut tart into 6 pieces and serve warm or at room temperature with vanilla ice cream or freshly whipped cream.

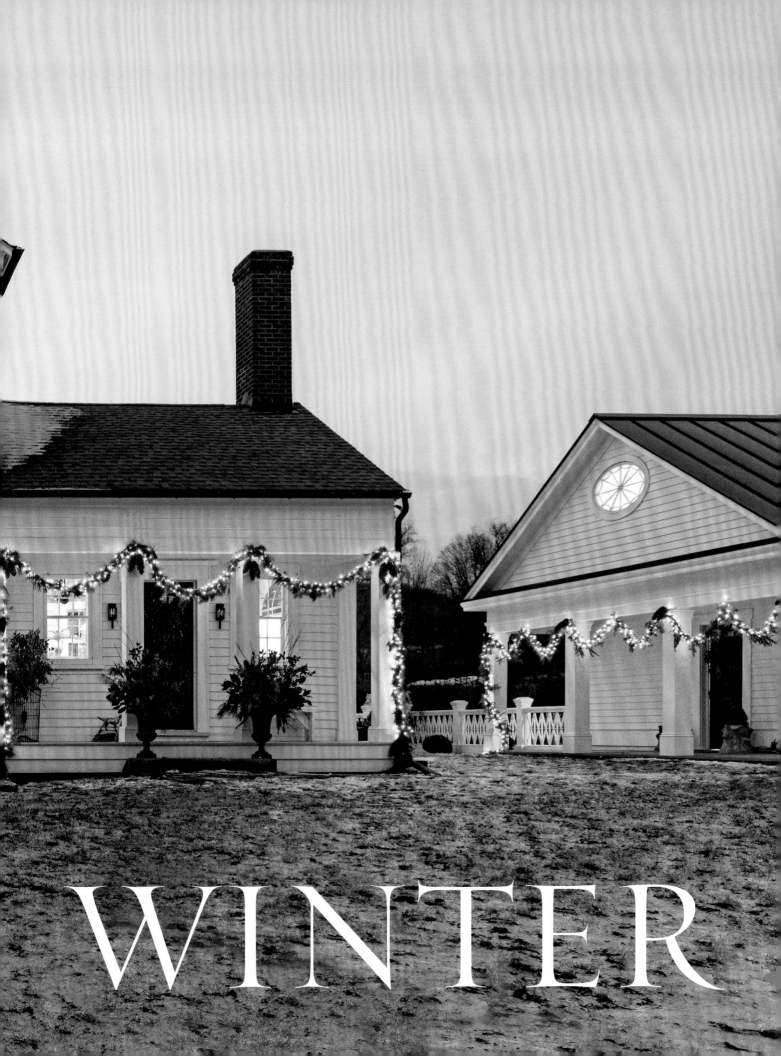

WINTER

DECEMBER

When you walk into some boutiques or department stores in the fall, holiday decorations are often being sold before Halloween. In some places, they appear just after Labor Day. As you've probably noticed throughout this book, I really like to get a jump start on whatever task is at hand, but at Clove Brook, the first week of December is the earliest you'll see any visible signs of Christmas cheer on view. I love the holidays. The ephemeral and fleeting nature of the season makes it worth savoring every single moment. I cherish my time with family and friends, although it is a busy month. My outdoor decor, which is composed of natural materials, mostly sourced from the surrounding area, offers a subtle hint of the exuberant mix of decorations indoors, in a riotous kaleidoscope of colors. In all, it takes me about a week to get everything decorated.

At my kitchen porch entrance, which is the one everybody uses when they visit the farm, I look to the giant and iconic flower arrangements in the Great Hall of the Metropolitan Museum of Art in New York City for inspiration. As you may know, they are towering designs created every week that loom high over visitors and are often photographed as much as the exhibitions. Their floral compositions regularly reach heights of twelve feet or more. Flanking my back entrance, a pair of large iron urns are the perfect vessels for my arrangements, albeit quite a bit smaller than the Met's. Still, they have a dynamic presence at a human scale. I start with magnolia branches as my foundation and add in red twig dogwood, vibrant clusters of crimson winterberry, and lacy boughs of

PREVIOUS PAGES: Dusk comes early at the farm in December—around 4:30 P.M.—so the interiors' warm glow is a welcoming sight, particularly when it's reflected on a light dusting of snow.
OPPOSITE: Fanny and I enjoy a tromp through freshly fallen snow, which is always a welcome addition during the holidays. Simple swags of white pine adorn the front porch.

"Happy, happy Christmas, that can win us back to the delusions of our childhood days, recall to the old man the pleasures of his youth, and transport the traveler back to his own fireside and quiet home!" —*Charles Dickens*

Norway pine. The mix has so many unique textures, I can eschew other adornments, such as ribbons or lights. Anything that I can source from the farm or nearby in Millbrook feels authentic because it truly is, and my guests pick up on those special gestures. For my front-door wreaths, which are placed to delight passersby along my country lane, I love to incorporate dried fruits, such as peaches and pomegranates, and I always look for a colored ribbon for my bows that's not the ubiquitous red or green or silver or gold, but a hue that still evokes the spirit of the season. I've had rich, golden yellows (almost a turmeric color), peacock blues, and even decadent plums. Fresh garlands draped on the dovecote and around the front columns are adorned with foot-long sugar pine cones for additional punctuation. Their overscale size gives them almost an architectural feeling. Where I choose to mix in decorative twinkling lights changes from season to season. Some years, I intertwine them on boxwoods and arrangements; other times I reserve them for garlands alone. The challenge is always figuring out when to stop.

OPPOSITE: At my kitchen entrance, guests are greeted by a pair of urns overflowing with magnolia branches, red twig dogwood, clusters of winterberry, and boughs of Norway pine. I was inspired by the majestic flower arrangements in the Metropolitan Museum of Art's Great Hall and wanted to create something substantial here. FOLLOWING PAGES: A Norway pine garland wrapped in twinkling lights illuminates the dovecote. The tall European hornbeam hedge retains its dead leaves all winter, offering privacy and architectural interest year-round.

OPPOSITE AND ABOVE: Colored ribbons adorn my collection of garden ornaments and wreaths. Aqua, golden yellow, aubergine, and crimson hues rotate from spot to spot each season, so no two years are exactly alike.

CHRISTMAS DECORATING

Every room in my house gets decorated for Christmas. I have the main tree in the living room, but large gestures and small touches continue throughout every space in the house—even the powder room gets a special something. I always joke that I love a scrawny, Charlie Brown–style tree. Sometimes I choose silvertip fir trees that I source from a shop in Connecticut, but most often it's a white pine that I find growing in the woods near my house. I prefer a Christmas tree that isn't so full and lush, because the empty space between the branches allows for oversize ornaments, such as my treasured 1930s glass icicles, to hang beautifully and not get lost in a sea of greenery. For illumination, I use a profusion of copper wire lights, which are wrapped tightly around each branch. I am often asked how many lights there are on my tree, yet I inevitably lose track—though it's almost always well over two thousand.

I was lucky to receive a box full of ornaments from the estate of my late friend Mario Buatta, and like most of the other pieces I place on my tree, they have a sentimental connection. Ornaments aren't just for the tree, however, and I also love to hang giant antique German glass kugels in many of my windows. The sunlight reflecting off the colored glass is dazzling. In addition to my tree, the fireplace mantel in my living room is another place where I like to focus a lot of attention. I decorate it with draped garlands composed of a mix of magnolia, Norway pine, and cedar branches, as well as sugar pine cones. Potted amaryllises flank a mirror of my own design, bringing yet another touch of the outdoors inside. Elsewhere throughout the house, carved Santa sculptures, tinsel trees, and gingerbread houses are placed, while the stockings are hung, awaiting Santa's arrival.

ABOVE: My mother first started buying carved wooden Santas made by artisans in western New York in the 1970s. We both have now amassed large collections of them. **OPPOSITE**: The living room's holiday regalia is a mix of all the things I adore: fresh greenery, decorative and artisanal objects made by hand, and items with personal meaning. The hooked zebra rug is from the former New York apartment of my friend and mentor, Albert Hadley. Coincidentally, the buildings shown in his sketchbook are reminiscent of the dovecote I built at the farm. The rug below is seagrass matting from Harbour Island in the Bahamas.

OPPOSITE: A gingerbread house is a mainstay of my Christmas decor. Every year, I gather with friends at a party to decorate our respective creations. ABOVE: Sturdy silvertip fir trees have a beautiful silhouette, but they are sparse, which makes them ideal for Christmas decorating. Tall ornaments and swags of garlands can hang beautifully off of their layered branches.

RIGHT: Embroidered stockings are festooned with a glitter pine cone-and-pecan garland.
PREVIOUS PAGES: The library's holiday decorations are a bit more demure than the living room's, but no less festive. A whimsical paper garland of Santa and his reindeer hangs between two windows and a pair of antique gold and green kugel ornaments. The biggest assemblage of my carved Santa collection resides on the coffee table. The owl painting above the mantel is by Van Day Truex.

ABOVE: Not all holiday decorations have to be elaborate in scale or execution. A small vintage feather tree conjures a smile in the master bedroom. **OPPOSITE**: Marian McEvoy designed the decorative collages, cork mirror, and lampshade. The mix of riotous patterns echoes the whimsical nature of the D. Porthault bed linens.

The Allure of Alliums

As I begin my holiday decorating, one of my first tasks is to head out to the barn to collect the bunches of alliums that I harvested back in July. The plant is a perennial that has fallen in and out of favor over the years. Allium is actually the Latin word for garlic, and it's included in the same family as chives, shallots, scallions, and leeks. They are also referred to as ornamental onions. I most often plant 'Purple Sensation', 'Gladiator', and 'Mount Everest' varieties, which feature giant purple and white ball-shaped flower heads. They look like fireworks exploding in air, and some of my plants grow as tall as five feet. I've found success by not overcrowding the bulbs when planting. Each bloom makes such a statement, and their impressive stature gets lost when they're bunched together. When cutting them for future arranging, wait until they are spent and their stalks start to brown at the ground. Then, put them in a bucket and dry them vertically so you don't damage their dried flower heads. The blooms have delicate features yet are pretty sturdy. Still, you don't want to risk damaging any of them by laying them flat. As I get ready to decorate for the holidays, I take mine to the field and give them a good coating of spray paint in lustrous gold and silver hues. This glittering effect highlights the beauty of their silhouettes. I then arrange them in one of my faux-bois urns surrounded by fresh-cut camellias. Their simple green leaves are the perfect foil for the alliums' metallic glow.

ABOVE, FROM LEFT: Alliums are larger than life—actually, the 'Mount Everest' variety is almost as tall as I am! Each dried bloom gets a quick coat of silver or gold spray paint. A close-up reveals the magical, metallic results. **OPPOSITE**: The dark green, glossy, and lush foliage of camellia branches is the perfect quiet backdrop to showcase the lustrous sparkle of the 'Gladiator' and 'Purple Sensation' allium blooms that have been painted gold and silver, respectively.

A CHRISTMAS LAP DINNER

Christmas gatherings are rituals I look forward to every year. On the second Saturday of each December, I host a holiday buffet dinner for close friends and neighbors. My mom even drives down from Buffalo for the festivities. Because there are usually a number of other cocktail parties happening that night, I don't do a formal sit-down dinner, and guests are able to come and go as they please. To prepare for the evening, I begin by cranking up the music—a jazzy Eartha Kitt number establishes a jovial mood for sorting the china, selecting napkins, hand-washing the crystal glasses, and polishing the silver. All of the food is set out in the kitchen before guests arrive. The main courses and side dishes shift from year to year—though comfort food always reigns supreme—but the sweets are the undeniable stars of the evening. Guests are greeted by a punch bowl brimming with homemade mulled wine and a big batch of eggnog whipped up from eggs gathered at the farm. Soft snowflake-shaped butter cookies melt in your mouth. An indulgent two-foot-long chocolate ganache Yule log, made

from a childhood recipe, is adorned with meringue mushrooms dusted with cocoa powder.

This is an informal evening, and everyone prepares his or her own plate for a lap dinner and finds a perch upon which to sit and mingle. I bring in extra seating that can be moved around from room to room, including garden stools and benches. For those who do gather around the available seats at the dining table, they are greeted by one of my antique birdcages serving as the centerpiece (the pigeons are returned to the dovecote before dinner is served), as well as arrangements of grapes, Meyer lemons, pomegranates, and miniature pine cones clustered in a pair of my faux-bois footed bowls. Anemones in bud vases are scattered down the table, but the fruit compositions show that flowers don't always have to be a mainstay when it comes to tabletop decor. With just a little adornment, simple fruits can be elevated and beautifully presented, especially when fresh flowers might not be in season or close at hand.

ABOVE: Setting the table. **OPPOSITE**: A papier-mâché orange by Wendy Addison graces the dining table for a holiday buffet dinner. If desired, it opens up to reveal a special treat—I've used several of her designs as place cards for seated dinners and filled them with pieces of chocolate—but it is an elegant, sculptural objet d'art on its own.

RIGHT: I bought the painted birdcage from an antiques dealer in Maine and adorned it with red velvet ribbons to serve as a centerpiece for my buffet dinner. Guests grab a seat at the table or anywhere throughout the house—the evening is an informal affair.

FOLLOWING PAGES, FROM LEFT: Star-topped cardboard glitter trees and a cornucopia of fruits in a cachepot of my design. My beloved pigeons make a cameo appearance during cocktail hour, before dinner is served.

RIGHT: Antique julep cups and emerald champagne flutes are ready to hold spirits, including homemade eggnog, champagne, and mulled-wine punch.

FOLLOWING PAGES: The festive yule log is based on a recipe that my mom used when I was growing up. The tree-shaped sponge cake is topped with a chocolate ganache and adorned with meringue mushrooms that I've stippled with cocoa powder.

ABOVE: Stacks of thin, crisp chocolate-chip cookies are elegantly presented on a clear glass cake stand. **OPPOSITE, CLOCKWISE FROM TOP LEFT**: Soft butter cookies are adorned with white buttercream icing and silver sprinkles. Oranges are displayed in a 1930s Constance Spry mantel vase, and the garland is composed of an assortment of unshelled nuts. Fresh eggs from my chickens are incorporated into the eggnog, including its fluffy whipped topping. When I don't use bamboo stakes to stabilize my potted paperwhites, I love gathering them with a beautiful satin or grosgrain ribbon. **FOLLOWING PAGES**: Having a collection of ribbons on hand keeps me from needing to run to the store to wrap a last-minute gift. In lieu of using printed wrapping papers that are holiday-specific, I keep an assortment of colored tissue paper handy, which can be used year-round for any holiday or celebration. I like using gift tags that have a vintage feeling with illustrations of engravings or etchings, and a sprig of fresh greenery is always a nice accompaniment.

TO:
Ashley
FROM:
Christopher

JANUARY/FEBRUARY

If there are any extended moments of stillness and quiet at the farm, they usually come during the first part of the new year. This is the time for reflecting on the whirl of the holidays that passed too quickly, as well as for gathering my thoughts and ideas for the year ahead. Although planning at the farm happens year-round, January 1 offers a blank page for stopping to recalibrate, and it's a great time for making lists. Lots of lists, in fact: new seeds that I want to source, other gardeners I want to meet, plant nurseries I want to visit. I am always excited to learn from new vendors and resources that never fail to inspire me. At this time, most of my gardening is happening indoors, and I usually have a few pots of crocuses, snowdrops, and hyacinths blooming on the windowsills and scattered elsewhere through the house. I planted those bulbs back in October, and their blooms offer pops of color when the days are short and gray.

This is also the time that I order honeybees for my hives. Mine are sourced from a grower in the Carolinas and shipped directly through the United States Postal Service to my local post office. They arrive in a small screened box just as the temperatures begin to warm up and are always a conversation starter when I go to fetch them at the postmaster's counter! Near the end of February, I start my tomato plants from seed out in the garage and order my bare-root roses from David Austin in England. The company offers what some people refer to as "old-fashioned" roses, which really means they have unique colors, petals, and scents that have since been bred out of many newer varieties. With good timing, both will be ready in time for planting outdoors in a couple of months. And believe it or not, I also find this time of year to be ideal for entertaining. People have more time on their hands after the holidays, and a good potluck or casual gathering for drinks and canapés is the perfect antidote to cabin fever.

Potted amaryllis adds a sculptural presence to any room. Bulbs take about six to eight weeks to bloom and require little attention. Because of their striking vertical stance, they don't take up much room, and you can tuck a pot of them in a tight space—atop a garden stool, on a mantel, even on a narrow powder room vanity.

Valentine's Dinner

Going out to dinner on Valentine's Day is often too much of a production, with limited seatings at restaurants and rigid prix fixe menus. I'd much rather cook a candlelight meal at home for Anthony and myself and include some of our favorite comfort foods. For a change of scenery, I love setting a table for the two of us at the desk in my living room. By contrast, my formal dining table is designed to accommodate twelve people, so it seems a bit stiff when it's just the two of us eating there alone. And while the kitchen table is quite cozy, it isn't terribly romantic. The desk, once belonging to legendary designer Keith Irvine, provides a perfect perch; plus, the chairs are really comfortable and there's a roaring fire just a few feet away. The table's supple leather top features an embossed gold border around the edge, so it doesn't need much adornment. A

tablecloth would feel contrived, so I selected two place mats made from a vintage Albert Hadley–designed fabric. Plates of my own design are based on a historic Wedgwood pattern that I interpreted. A small arrangement of purple anemones and red ranunculus packs a visual punch, and the colors are reflected in my monogrammed napkins from Leontine Linens. Anthony and I share a simple roast chicken—a recipe that I've developed with my mother over the years—along with cauliflower mash, sautéed spinach with garlic and lemon, and chocolate mousse for dessert. Of course, it has to be chocolate—some traditions are worth adhering to! As the sun sets early on this winter day, one of my lamps from my collection with Visual Comfort is illuminated to cast a soft glow on this quiet setting as gifts are exchanged.

ABOVE: A Valentine's gift is wrapped in teal tissue paper and adorned with a cranberry-colored ribbon. **OPPOSITE**: My Ralphaeli lamp for Visual Comfort was inspired by a Giacometti design and rests atop a desk formerly owned by designer Keith Irvine. Painted Louis XVI–style chairs are upholstered in brown leather and outlined with red ribbon trim and brass nailheads. The decorative ceramic cat, and the stool upon which it rests, once belonged to Sister Parish. **FOLLOWING PAGES**: Purple anemones and red ranunculus **(RIGHT)** reflect the garnet-colored glassware and linen napkins **(LEFT)**. A collection of porcelain fruits by my friend Clare Potter is accompanied by another bowl of antique ceramic peas.

LIVING WITH DOGS

While I have a menagerie of farm animals outdoors, I can't imagine my life at Clove Brook without my two dogs. Fanny, a Cavalier King Charles spaniel, and Lyon, a black Labrador retriever, add so much vitality to farm life. Their joyful spirits are contagious, and life before them seemed unusually quiet, both literally and figuratively. (Fanny may clock in at a mere twenty pounds, but she is an epic snorer!) I strive to give them as much unconditional love and companionship as they give me. In short, they are spoiled! They have cozy and cushy beds in the kitchen, where everyone congregates, as well as crates upstairs in the master bedroom. From time to time, Fanny gets in the bed for an occasional morning snuggle, but since she and Lyon have been crate trained, they consider those beds their safe spaces and retreat to

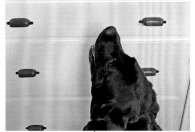

them without any hesitation. Their diet is made up of a basic organic kibble, which is occasionally supplemented with no- to low-salt treats, primarily extra leftover chicken or vegetable scraps. I follow my veterinarian's recommendations for regular care and checkups, and thankfully, both love to be active. Frolicking and exploring in the snow this time of year is a favorite pastime—quilted jackets help them retain their body heat—and an assortment of toys keeps them in high spirits and encourages activity when it's too cold to go outside for extended periods of time. Although the farm affords them acres to explore, I don't let them wander to the far reaches of the property unattended—predators such as coyotes are real threats to their safety, so I accompany them or keep a very close eye on them from the house.

ABOVE: Lyon, always eager for a meal. **OPPOSITE**: Because they were socialized early as puppies, Lyon, my Labrador retriever, and Fanny, my Cavalier King Charles spaniel, get along with other dogs and easily adapt to urban living in New York City during the week and country living at Clove Brook Farm on the weekends.

WELCOMING GUESTS

If you create a simple process for making sure rooms are always ready for guests, even at a moment's notice, you'll never have to worry if the medicine cabinet is stocked with sundries or if there are towels that need to be laundered. Because staying overnight at a friend's house can be like a mini vacation, I wanted to indulge my guests and create joyful spaces for them that are probably a departure from how they live day to day. Even compared to the colorful rooms in my home's public spaces on the first floor, the exuberant wallpapers in the guest rooms are a graphic notch above the rest. Unlike in everyday spaces, where you might tire of a particular pattern, rooms used on a short-term basis allow you to be a bit more daring with your design. Plus, I wanted the guest rooms in the attic to feel as plush and detailed as my own, which they are.

Creating a comfortable bed is of utmost importance for overnighters. I love dressing the bed with whimsical printed linens from D. Porthault, exquisite hand-monogrammed

designs from Leontine Linens, and the crisp whites from Schweitzer. After the linens are laundered, I always have them pressed with a scented lavender water. In bath cupboards, I stock the shelves with the basics, such as soaps, shampoos, and mouthwash, but also earplugs and sleep masks. Bedside tables are adorned with a simple arrangement of flowers or a single flower in a bud vase. There's always a carafe or bottle of water. When all of the rooms are full, I set the breakfast table in the kitchen before I go to bed and leave ground coffee on the counter so the first person to rise can start the first of what promise to be many brewed pots.

The most important thing is that my guests have plenty of room to stow their own clothes, so it's imperative that the dresser cabinets and closet racks are cleared out. I would love to have those spaces as extra storage for myself, but I always keep them spare or empty, as I've been a guest in other people's houses without an inch of space to put my own things. I want my guests to settle in and make themselves right at home.

ABOVE: With one of my favorite ceramic hares perched nearby, overnight guests always have company. **OPPOSITE**: Leading into one of the guest rooms, the closets on the right are left spare to accommodate friends' luggage and hanging clothes.

ABOVE: Task and accent lighting is a must for any bedroom. My friend Clare Potter and I collaborated on the design of this lamp, which is covered in ceramic flowers. **OPPOSITE, CLOCKWISE FROM TOP LEFT**: A slipper chair offers a place for respite. Each guest room is stocked with a tray of bottled waters, ice, and fresh lemon. A small pitcher of red anemones graces a bedside table. The owl print is one of a pair formerly owned by Albert Hadley that I refashioned in a tramp art frame. **FOLLOWING PAGES**: The Fireworks wallpaper pattern, designed by Hadley, brings a jolt of energy and levity to the attic guest room. The window seat offers visitors a nice perch for reading or napping.

OPPOSITE: In the main guest suite and other guest rooms, I make sure that each space features the same creature comforts I have in my own bedroom, including down pillows and duvets, ironed linens, and a perch for reading or relaxing. **ABOVE**: When I have just one overnight guest, I love to treat the person to a simple breakfast tray. A blueberry muffin, fresh hard-boiled eggs, and a Christofle silver carafe filled with piping-hot coffee allow my guest to have a languorous start to the day. My blue-and-white Marble ceramics and D. Porthault linens accent the rattan tray.

229

WINTER BLOOMS

I have friends who tell me they don't have a green thumb and are intimidated to attempt gardening. I encourage them to buy a houseplant or grow some vegetables in containers outside, even if they only have a tiny apartment balcony. Start small and see how it goes. Like novice cooks who begin by attempting complicated recipes, overly ambitious gardeners are the ones who often get disillusioned if their first attempts don't go according to plan. Forcing bulbs in water is one of my other favorite techniques that I suggest for introductory gardening, particularly at this time of year, when it's cold outside. The process is practically foolproof.

Because the bottoms of the bulbs are barely submerged in water and we aren't using soil, the exercise feels a bit like a fun science experiment. In fact, it is a hydroponic way of growing. Forcing bulbs means that you are persuading them to bloom when you want. Paperwhite and amaryllis bulbs are the standard-bearers. When you buy them at the store, they are ready to be planted immediately. Hyacinth bulbs, on the other hand, need to be refrigerated for about eight weeks or longer. Your garden center can advise you on chilling times. You can force bulbs in almost any sort of container that holds water; if it has a bit of a bowl shape, even better. I love using a tall blue-and-white pedestal bowl of my own design. The bowl is filled with about half an inch of water and a thin layer of antique glass marbles, and the paperwhite bulbs are nestled into the nooks and crannies, with the tip of each bulb barely grazing the water. I start new pots of bulbs every two weeks to have a constant rotation of blossoms throughout the winter. Just as one arrangement is fading, another is ready to take its place. They are reminders that hope springs eternal and that Mother Nature will soon cast her warmth on the bulbs planted outside.

OPPOSITE: The swirling pattern of the footed pedestal I designed echoes the patterns found in the marbles. **ABOVE, FROM LEFT**: My collection of vintage marbles. The bottom tips of the paperwhite bulbs graze the water through the nooks and crannies of the marbles. Each bulb and marble is placed one at a time to secure the plants in place. **FOLLOWING PAGES**: My collection of new and vintage jewel-toned hyacinth bulb forcers. The blooms of the 'Woodstock' (magenta—my favorite), 'Aiolos' (white), 'Fondant' (pink), and 'Aida' (purple) hyacinths produce a heady fragrance.

WINTER CALENDAR

DECEMBER

Christmas decorating begins the first week of the month.

Host annual Christmas party the second Saturday.

Keep track of how many feet of garland I buy every year, particularly in new areas.

Spray-paint allium heads for holiday decor.

Clean and service farm equipment.

Add a generous amount of mulch around the bases of the rosebushes.

Wrap gifts at least one week ahead of Christmas. The wrapping is as important as the gift, and you don't want to spend your Christmas Eve in a panic.

JANUARY & FEBRUARY

Recycle Christmas tree and garlands.

Force hyacinth bulbs for indoor blooming.

Tend to the plants in the garage; adjust the timing of grow lights to mimic the season.

Order honeybees and roses for spring delivery.

Sharpen garden tools.

Stock guest rooms with bottled water, stationery, current magazines, fresh soap, and toiletries. Add plants and flowers when guests arrive.

Propagate new plants, such as salvia, verbena, and figs. Coat the stem cuttings in rooting hormone before planting in a pot. Place in a sunny location and water regularly.

Check wild-bird feeders and refill as necessary.

Review garden journals and notebooks from previous years for reference and inspiration.

In February, prune apple trees on a sunny day. Cut off all of the vertical growth on the branches so that air can circulate.

GIFT OF THE SEASON

Although I harvest honey at the farm in the fall, it stores extremely well and is the ideal go-to present for last-minute holiday parties, friends, and acquaintances. On most of my gifts, custom labels featuring an illustration of the farmhouse add a personalized touch.

BETTER THAN RESTAURANT ROAST CHICKEN
Serves 4

I developed this recipe with my mother, Amy Mayfield. Everyone loves it. It's amazing how much flavor you can get from so few ingredients. I suggest buying a good-quality local chicken or one from Bell & Evans.

  I 4–5 lb. whole chicken

  Fine sea salt

  2 Tbsp. extra-virgin olive oil

I. Rinse chicken inside and out with cold running water. Towel-dry and salt all over. (I start with the back, then the cavity, then the breast, legs, and wings until the entire chicken is evenly salted.)

2. Place chicken, uncovered, on a plate in your refrigerator for at least 8 hours and up to 24. This process is essentially a dry brine.

3. Remove chicken from refrigerator and blot any excess water from it to ensure crispy skin.

4. Preheat oven to 450°F.

5. Heat oil in a 10-inch cast-iron skillet over high heat until just smoking. Sear chicken breast-side down for 7 to 10 minutes, until skin is very dark brown and turns black in spots. (You may think the bird is burned, but it's not.)

6. Turn chicken over and repeat process breast-side up.

7. Place skillet in oven and roast for approximately 45 minutes, or until juices run clear and the internal temperature of the thigh reaches 165°F.

8. Let chicken rest for 10 minutes before carving.

NOTE: To serve, I like to use poultry scissors to cut the roasted bird into 8 pieces. First, I cut out the backbone. Then I remove the legs and thighs, cutting them each into 2 pieces at the drumstick. The wing remains attached to the breast, and the breast meat is cut into halves (one with the wing attached), creating 8 pieces in all. This way, you can serve four people, and everyone can select the piece of chicken he or she prefers.

THE BEST CHOCOLATE CHIP COOKIES
Makes 30 cookies

  2 sticks salted butter, at room temperature

  I cup dark brown sugar, firmly packed

  I cup granulated sugar

  2 large eggs, at room temperature

  I Tbsp. real vanilla extract

  I tsp. baking soda

  2 tsp. salt

  I ½ cups all-purpose flour

  24 oz. bittersweet chocolate chips

I. Preheat oven to 375°F.

2. In a stand mixer with the whisk attachment, combine butter and sugars on medium speed until light and creamy, about 3 to 5 minutes.

3. Add one egg at a time, then the vanilla extract. Use a spatula to scrape down the sides of the bowl.

4. Add baking soda, salt, and flour slowly. When just incorporated, turn off mixer and fold in chocolate chips.

5. Place dough in teaspoon-size mounds on a baking sheet lined with parchment paper.

6. Bake cookies for 10 to 12 minutes, rotating pan halfway. Remove when cookies are brown at the edges but still soft in the center.

7. Cool on baking sheet for 7 to 10 minutes before transferring to a wire rack or plate.

Resources

ANTIQUES SHOWS

Antiques & Garden Show of Nashville, *antiquesandgardenshow.com*

Barn Star's Antiques at Rhinebeck, *barnstar.com*

Birmingham Botanical Gardens' Antiques at the Gardens, *bbgardens.org/antiques*

Blue Grass Trust for Historic Preservation's Antiques & Garden Show, *bluegrasstrust.org*

Charleston Antiques Show, *historiccharleston.org*

The Nantucket Summer Antiques Show, *nantucketsummerantiquesshow.com*

The San Francisco Fall Show, *sffallshow.org*

AUCTION HOUSES

Doyle, *doyle.com*
Stair Galleries, *stairgalleries.com*

BEEKEEPING
Hive Kits
Kelley Beekeeping, *kelleybees.com*

Supplies
Betterbee, *betterbee.com*

CHRISTOPHER SPITZMILLER LAMPS AND ACCESSORIES STOCKISTS

100 Main, *100mainst.com*

Abino Mills, *abinomills.com*

Ainsworth-Noah, *ainsworth-noah.com*

Allison Caccoma, *allisoncaccoma.com*

Antonio's Bella Casa, *antoniosbellacasa.com*

Benjamin Deaton Interior Design, *benjamindeatondesign.com*

Christopher Spitzmiller, *christopherspitzmiller.com*

Circa Lighting, *circalighting.com*

Darnell & Co., *darnellandcompany.com*

Eric Haydel, *erichaydel.com*

Fanny Bolen Interiors, *fannyboleninteriors.com*

FOUND For the Home, *foundforthehome.com*

G&G Interiors, *gg-interiors.com*

Hive, *hivepalmbeach.com*

Jasper, *michaelsmithinc.com/jasper-showroom*

John Rosselli Antiques, *johnrosselliantiques.com*

Karen Harlow for the Home, *karenharlowforthehome.com*

KRB, *krbnyc.com*

Longoria Collection, *longoriacollection.com*

Mathews Furniture & Design, *mathewsfurniture.com*

Mecox, *mecox.com*

Monica James & Co., *monicajames.com*

Newport Lamp and Shade, *newportlampandshade.com*

Paloma & Co, *shoppalomaandco.com*

Pecky, *peckysrq.com*

The Shade Shop, *theshadeshop.com*

Shaun Smith Home, (504) 896-1020

CUSTOM FABRICS

Tillett Textiles, *t4fabrics.com*
Zina Studios, *zinastudios.com*

FLOWERS
Dahlias
Bear Creek Farm, *bearcreekfarm.com*
Ferncliff Gardens, *ferncliffgardens.com*
Swan Island Dahlias, *dahlias.com*

Lilies
B & D Lilies, *bdlilies.com*
Van Engelen Inc., *vanengelen.com*

Narcissi and Other Bulbs
Brent and Becky's, *brentandbeckysbulbs.com*
Colorblends, *colorblends.com*
Van Engelen Inc., *vanengelen.com*

Peonies
Cricket Hill Garden, *treepeony.com*
Peony's Envy, *peonysenvy.com*
Song Sparrow, *songsparrow.com*

Roses
David Austin Roses, *davidaustinroses.com*
Heirloom Roses, *heirloomroses.com*

Specialty Flower and Vegetable Seeds
Floret, *floretflowers.com*
Johnny's Selected Seeds, *johnnyseeds.com*

Sweet Peas
Ardelia Farm & Co., *ardeliafarm.com*
Owl's Acre Seed, *owlsacreseeds.co.uk*

GARDEN TOOLS
Pruners
A.M. Leonard, *amleo.com*
Tetsufuku, *tetsufuku.com*

Standing Sprinklers
Gilmour, *gilmour.com*

LOCAL PROVISIONS AND SPECIALTY FOOD STORES
Double L Market, *doublelmarket.com*

The Market at Mabbettsville,
themarketatmabbettsville.com

Quattro's Farm Store, (845) 635-2018

NURSERIES
Foliage Garden, *foliagegarden.com*
Orangerie Garden, *orangeriegarden.com*
Snug Harbor Farm, *snugharborfarm.com*
Surry Gardens, *surrygardens.com*

POULTRY BREEDER
Hubbell Spring Farm, *hubbellspringfarm.com*

POULTRY SHOWS AND EXHIBITS
Northeastern Poultry Congress, *poultrycongress.com*
The Ohio National, *ohionational.org*

PRIVATE GARDEN TOURS
The Garden Conservancy, *gardenconservancy.org*

PUBLIC GARDENS
Innisfree Garden, *innisfreegarden.org*
Planting Fields, *plantingfields.org*
Stonecrop Gardens, *stonecrop.org*
Wave Hill, *wavehill.org*
Wethersfield, *wethersfield.org*

SEASONAL DECOR
Christmas Trees, Anemones, and Ranunculus
Abel's Trees, *abelstrees.com*
Battenfeld's Christmas Tree Farm,
christmastreefarm.us
Terrain, *shopterrain.com*

Gift Wrap
Fairhope Graphics, *fairhopegraphics.com*

Ribbon
May Arts, *mayarts.com*
Theatre of Dreams, *wendyaddisonstudio.com*

Ornaments
John Derian, *johnderian.com*
Matt McGhee, *mattmcghee.com*

STATIONERY
Atelier Benneton Graveur, *shop.bennetongraveur.com*
Mapleshade Press, *kristafragos.com*
The Printery, *iprintery.com*

TABLE AND BED LINENS
D. Porthault, *dporthaultparis.com*
John Robshaw, *johnrobshaw.com*
Leontine Linens, *leontinelinens.com*
Matouk, *matouk.com*

ACKNOWLEDGMENTS

I want to thank the following people, whose support and friendship mean the world to me.

Martha Stewart, who has inspired me since I was a kid when I laid my eyes on her first book, *Entertaining*. She has since become a great friend and mentor, and she encourages me to teach and inspire and share my own passions with others as well.

My grandfather John Goodell who taught me the importance of having my own business from an early age.

My mother, Amy Mayfield, from whom I got my style and flair for entertaining. My father, Robert F. Spitzmiller Jr., who gave me my strong work ethic. My brothers and sisters: Cameron Spitzmiller, Robert Spitzmiller, Lindsay Mayfield, and Lisa Spitzmiller.

Ashley Whittaker, who has become my adopted sister and the best friend one could ask for.

Harry Heissmann, who held my hand throughout the decoration process at Clove Brook Farm and taught me so much.

Richard Keith Langham, for ordering my very first lamps.

Clare Potter, Bunny Williams and John Rosselli, Page Dickey, Memrie Lewis, Stephen Sills, Carolyne Roehm, Cathy Graham, Ryan McCallister, and Arthur Parkinson, my gardening friends and inspiring talents.

Alex Papachristidis, Scott Nelson, Marian McEvoy, Hadley Scully, Natalie Leventhal, Emily Eerdmans, Christina Markey, Bruce Addison, Michael Foster, David Svanda, Seth Raphaeli, Todd Alexander Romano, and Sam Allen, for being true longtime friends.

Mac Hoak, Pat Grey, Jonathan Gargiulo, Kate Brodsky, Suzanne Rheinstein Brodsky, Karen Harlow, and Ruth and Neill Davis, for your enthusiasm and belief in what I do.

Andy Singer, Gale Singer, and the entire Visual Comfort and Circa Lighting families, for your support and collaboration.

Amy Astley, Steele Marcoux, Robert Rufino, Margaret Russell, Margot Shaw, Steven Stolman, and Stellene Volandes for publishing my work.

Gail Monaghan, Mimi Thorisson, and Julie "June Bug" Williamson, for sharing with me so many tricks in the kitchen.

Penny Matteson, for being my fairy godmother.

Mario Buatta, for mostly cheering me along.

Gemma and Andrew Ingalls, whose photography made Clove Brook Farm come alive.

My Rizzoli family, Charles Miers and Kathleen Jayes, as well as Jill Cohen, Doug Turshen, David Huang, Steve Walkowiak, and Clinton Smith, for making this dream book a reality.

Zaheer Nota, for being my third hand at the studio.

Thank you for the support of all my friends, employees, clients, stores, and decorators for making this book possible.

Lastly, to Clove Brook Farm, for giving me a sense of purpose, responsibility, and pride for fifteen years and counting.

First published in the United States of America in 2021 by
Rizzoli International Publications, Inc.
300 Park Avenue South
New York, NY 10010
www.rizzoliusa.com

Text: Clinton Smith
Foreword: Martha Stewart

All photography by Gemma & Andrew Ingalls except:
Page 6 lower right, 181, 187: Melanie Acevedo
28–29, 96: Quentin Bacon
116–117, 220: Christopher Spitzmiller
189: Anthony Bellomo

Developed in collaboration with Jill Cohen Associates, LLC.

Publisher: Charles Miers
Senior Editor: Kathleen Jayes
Design: Doug Turshen with David Huang
Production Manager: Alyn Evans
Managing Editor: Lynn Scrabis

Printed in China

2021 2022 2023 2024 / 10 9 8 7 6 5 4 3

ISBN: 978-0-8478-69749

Library of Congress Control Number: 2020947693

Visit us online:
Facebook.com/RizzoliNewYork
Twitter: @Rizzoli_Books
Instagram.com/RizzoliBooks
Pinterest.com/RizzoliBooks

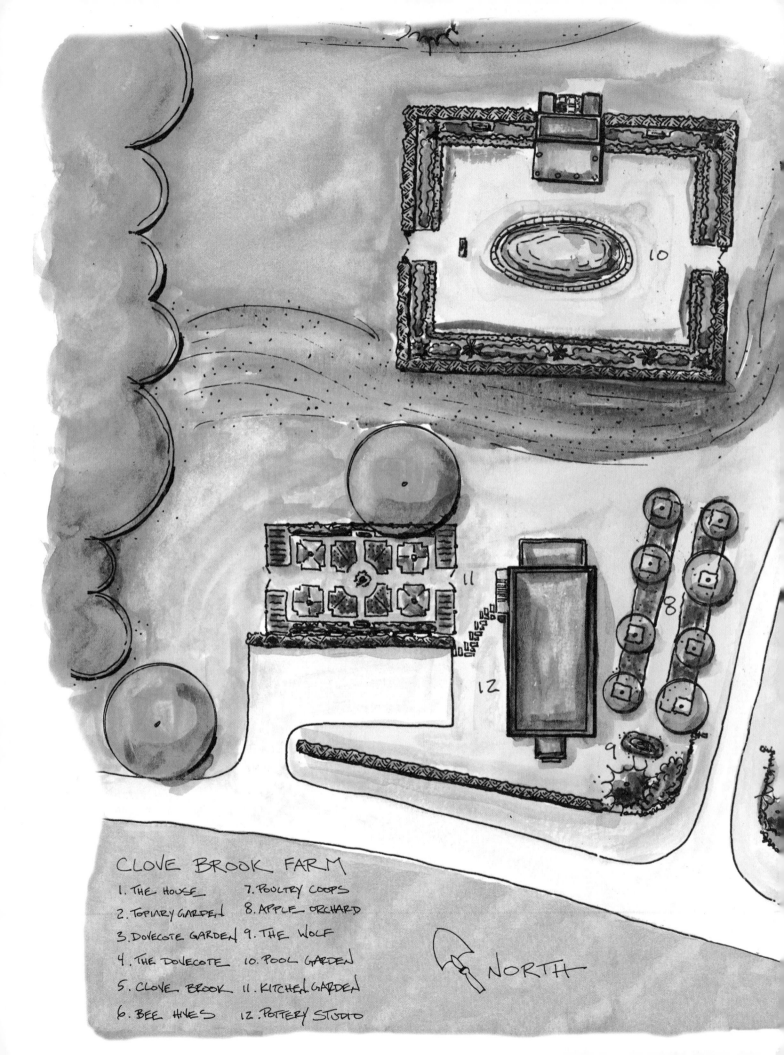

CLOVE BROOK FARM

1. THE HOUSE
2. TOPIARY GARDEN
3. DOVECOTE GARDEN
4. THE DOVECOTE
5. CLOVE BROOK
6. BEE HIVES
7. POULTRY COOPS
8. APPLE ORCHARD
9. THE WOLF
10. POOL GARDEN
11. KITCHEN GARDEN
12. POTTERY STUDIO

NORTH